THE PSYCHGEIST OF POP CULTURE

CULTURE

THE UMBRELLA ACADEMY

ARIENNE FERCHAUD, PHD

PLAY STORY PRESS

CONTENTS

Psychgeist Of Pop Culture Series   vii

There's No Such Thing As Good Guys Or Bad Guys,
There's Just People   1
Arienne Ferchaud, PhD

Tell Tale Hargreeves   5
Petrana Radulovic

Egad, A Talking Chimpanzee!   15
Jennifer Fuller, PhD

It's Not Me, It's You: Childhood Trauma's Impact On
Adult Sibling Relationships   35
Jasmine Heyward

Why Do We Not Love All The Hargreeves' Siblings
The Same?   57
Michelle Möri and Andreas Fahr

An Unlikely Pair: Five And Delores   73
Emory S. Daniel, PhD

Klaus The Kindly Cult Leader   87
Kelly Chernin, PhD

Reactionary Reactions? Fan Responses To Viktor's
Identity Development   109
Sofia V. Rhea and Laramie D. Taylor, PhD

Protagonists, Villain Protagonists, And Morality   127
Arienne Ferchaud, PhD

Systems, Roles, And Coping: A Case Study Of The
Hargreeves' Family   143
Shane Tilton, PhD

About the Editor   161
About The Authors   163
About Play Story Press   169

Created with Vellum

PSYCHGEIST OF POP CULTURE SERIES

Play Story Press
Pittsburgh, PA

Series Editor: Rachel Kowert, PhD

Over the last few decades interest in pop psychology has grown faster than our Netflix backlogs. This series highlights iconic pop culture content from television, film, literature, and video games through an examination of the psychological mechanisms that endear us to these stories for a lifetime.

SERIES TITLES

The Witcher (2023), edited by Rachel Kowert, PhD
The Mandalorian (2024), edited by Jessica E. Tompkins, PhD
The Umbrella Academy (2024), edited by Arienne Ferchaud, PhD

THERE'S NO SUCH THING AS GOOD GUYS OR BAD GUYS, THERE'S JUST PEOPLE

ARIENNE FERCHAUD, PHD

T he Umbrella Academy is more than just a story of extraordinary children. It is a poignant reflection on common human struggles – familial relationships, romantic relationships, and just want we would all be doing should the apocalypse befall our planet. The stories of the The Umbrella Academy first came to life in a series of comic books created and written by Gerard Way, illustrated by Gabriel Bá, and published by Dark Horse Comics. It was released as a six-issue limited series entitled The Umbrella Academy, Apocalypse Suite in 2007, with a second series The Umbrella Academy: Dallas being released the following year. The last iteration, The Umbrella Academy: Hotel Oblivion was released in across 2018 and 2019. Dark Horse Comics has also published four short stories from this universe. The television adaptation of The Umbrella Academy premiered on Netflix in February 2019 to rave reviews. In 2019, Netflix reported it was the third most watched series on their platform[1]. Today, the audience demand for the show remains at 16.4x the demand of the average TV series in the United States (at the time of this writing)[2].

The books and the Netflix series begin exactly the same way with

1

the birth of 43 extraordinary children, each born to women who had not, prior to that moment, been pregnant. These children are incredible, not only due to the circumstances of their birth, but the fact that they each possess superhuman abilities.

Seven of these children are adopted by eccentric billionaire Sir Reginald Hargreeves, who immediately begins the process of training them into an elite superhero team. The titular Umbrella Academy consists of:

- Number One: Luther/Spaceboy, who has superhuman strength.
- Number Two: Diego/The Kraken whose powers differ between the comics (in which he can hold his breath underwater indefinitely) and the show (in which he can control projectiles).
- Number Three: Allison/The Rumor, who has the ability to manipulate reality by speaking a sentence beginning with the phrase *"I heard a rumor..."*
- Number Four: Klaus/Séance, who can speak to and channel the dead.
- Number Five: The only Hargreeves sibling to never be referred to by name. Five has the ability to teleport through time and space.
- Number Six: Ben/The Horror, who can summon tentacles from an eldritch being living in an interdimensional space in his chest.
- Number Seven: Vanya/Viktor, who seems to have no powers at all. (Seven is called Viktor in the program, as the character transitioned along with his actor, Elliot Page)

We quickly learn that adoptive father Sir Reginald Hargreeves is an absent father at the best of the times and explicitly abusive at the worst. He refers to the children not by name, but by a ranking system that seems to organize children by their usefulness to the team. Number One, Luther, is the de facto leader, while Number Seven, Vanya/Viktor is considered to be the least useful due to an apparent lack of power. He also often pits the children against each other, which leads to building resentment between them as they compete for their father's approval. By the time the series begins, one sibling is dead, another is missing, and the remaining have scattered, barely speaking to each other.

While the crimefighting days of the Hargreeves' children are alluded to in flashbacks, they are *not* the focus of *The Umbrella Academy*. Rather, the series focuses on the lives of the children years later, after the academy has shut down. The children are reunited as many estranged families are—for a funeral. Sir Reginald has died, and the siblings, some of whom have not spoken in several years, return. They are prepared to return to their own individual lives when their missing brother Five appears in a portal, trapped in his childhood body, warning of an incoming apocalypse. Suddenly, the siblings are forced to confront their own issues and their familial dysfunction to end the worldwide threat.

In this series of collected essays, we explore the world of *The Umbrella Academy* through the lens of its characters, their psychology, and audience reactions. We will explore topics such as family trauma and its impact on adult sibling relationships, Kalus' cult leading days, Viktor's identity development, and the psychological processes that lead Five to fall in love with Dolores (if you know, you know). In the end, this collection hopes to highlight the universal lessons that can be taken from the (mis)adventures of the Hargreeves family: to love your family unconditionally, to forgive even in the face of betrayal, to always take a moment for the small wins and to look for hope in the face of an apocalypse.

NOTES

1. Littleton, C. (2019, December 30). Stranger Things 3, The Witcher, When they See Us, Among Netflix's Most Popular TV Shows in 2019. *Variety*. Retrieved from https://variety.com/2019/tv/news/netflix-most-popular-tv-series-2019-stranger-things-the-witcher- when-they-see-us-1203453295/
2. Parrot Analytics. (2024)., The Umbrella Academy. Retrieved form https://tv.parrotanalytics.com/US/the-umbrella-academy-netflix

TELL TALE HARGREEVES

PETRANA RADULOVIC

E xploring the Gothic Allure of the Umbrella Academy

AT TIMES, Netflix's take on *The Umbrella Academy* feels like it has more in common with the Gothic works of the Brontë sisters than it does with superhero tutelage.

Perhaps, given the series' pedigree, this isn't surprising. The comic series was penned by My Chemical Romance lead, Gerard Way, icon of alternative eyeliner and fingerless-glove wearing teenagers since 2001. But while there is overlap between Mall Goth and Romantic Goth, the elements of *The Umbrella Academy*'s first season that make it so distinct speak to the likes of Edgar Allan Poe, Mary Shelley, and the Brontë sisters.

The Netflix version[1] of the Hargreeves siblings could simply be another tale of superheroes living together and saving the world. But because the superpowers are treated more like elements of the preternatural, the landscape and aesthetic feel lifted from the pages of an 1800s Romance, and the characters feel less like superheroes and more like Byronic heroes, it offers a unique and captivating lens to the superhero genre. And like the Gothic novels of the 1800s, it posits a perfect alternative to the norms of the genre, diving into territory otherwise unexamined.

A DARK AND GLOOMY MANSION...

One of the biggest staples of Gothic literature is the setting. *Wuthering Heights*[2] wouldn't be *Wuthering Heights* without the vast Yorkshire moors and the titular estate. *Jane Eyre*[3] would be nothing without the halls of Thornfield Manor and that mysterious third floor. There's a reason why so many Gothic staples are named after places — *The Castle of Otranto!*[4] *The Romance of the Forest!*[5] The setting makes the story.

The Umbrella Academy follows in this grand tradition. The title speaks not just to the Hargreeves siblings themselves, but the physical location of the academy. In the first season particularly, most of the story takes place within its gloomy walls, where there are few, if any, happy memories within those shadowed hallways.

There is the study that Reginald holed himself inside that the children were never allowed to enter and still carefully tread around in his passing, though they are full grown adults. There are the halls full of paintings that Grace, their robot caretaker, gazes longingly at, knowing that they are all glimpses of an outside world she will never get to see. There's a cemetery in the backyard, where young Klaus had to confront restless spirits without fully understanding his own powers.

With its high ceilings and wrought-iron decor, the Academy feels more like a tomb than a home, burying the siblings under the weight of their past. And that would absolutely fit the Gothic conventions. Edgar Allen Poe's *The Fall of the House of Usher*[6] involves a man burying his sister alive in the family tomb.

From a purely aesthetic sense, the macabre surroundings are pleasing to the eye; there's something intoxicating and compelling about the dark set dressing. After all, it *is* a nice house, part Upper East Side brownstone, part Vanderbilt manor. But even in its grandness, the Hargreeves house is framed off puttingly, enough to build that sense of unease and cement the fact that none of the Hargreeves really want to be there. But the stony and austere facade of the academy also gives the overarching themes of the show a tangibility. When the past is made tangible in the form of a house, it is all the harder to escape.

That is why there are so many iconic houses in Gothic literature. They're physical manifestations of the bigger themes in the text, be it the primal passion of the Yorkshire moors in *Wuthering Heights*, or decay and stagnation in *The Fall of the House of Usher*. In *The Umbrella Academy*, the Hargreeves house is a haunting reminder of the Hargreeves' siblings upbringing, the past that they cannot escape no matter how far they run, how much they reinvent themselves. When they leave the house, it represents drastic change, both good and bad. And still, they're drawn back into its walls, reverting right back to their old habits.

BYRONIC HEROES, GALORE

A staple of the Romantic and Gothic periods, the Byronic hero is grandfather of all the brooding anti-heroes out there[7]. There are plenty of modern superheroes who also share a sulking, woeful personality and tragic pasts. But the key difference is, save for Diego, none of the Hargreeves are picking up masks and fighting crime. They emulate the characteristics of the Byronic hero first, the super-powers an afterthought.

Named for poet Lord Byron, these original bad boys have a bit more 19th century woe than 21st century angst than a hero like Batman. And back in the 19th century, antihero characters like this were distinct for going against the noble and heroic grain. They showcased darker characteristics of humanity, which was just as appealing then as it is now.

Today, it's common to see edgy antiheroes across television and movies (and one could argue, even more so than regular, straight-laced heroes). But what sets *The Umbrella Academy* apart is how closely the main cast can check qualities off the original Byronic hero list: they struggle with complex emotions; feel a certain degree of isolation; and they balance their self-destructive behavior with magnetic appeal. Basically all of the Hargreeves siblings share *some* key traits with the archetypal Byronic hero, but Luther and Diego fill the trope the best, with Allison highlighting a rare female example.

Duty-bound Luther struggles to fulfill his father's wishes, while feeling he has the body of a monster. While many Byronic heroes are roguishly handsome, there's also a subset that view themselves as physically unattractive. Luther's bizarre body situation certainly brings to mind Frankenstein's monster and the Phantom of the Opera, but he also very specifically has physical traits shared by *Jane Eyre*'s Mr. Rochester ("granite- hewn features" and "unusual breadth of chest, disproportionate almost to his length of limb.") In the first season especially, Luther tortures himself over his duty to his family and what he wants, and ultimately that struggle is what contributes directly to the end of the world. And just like *Wuthering Heights*' Heathcliff, the quintessential Byronic hero who contributes to his own family's destruction, Luther's got it down bad for an adopted sister. (Thankfully, Luther gets over that).

Diego goes in the opposite direction, shunning the family name to fuel his own quest for justice. He's cockier than Luther, not afraid to go against the rules and the grain of society (so much so, that he got kicked out of police academy). Unlike Luther, his Byronic arc is focused more on vengeance, ala the titular character in *The Count of Monte Cristo*. It's more external, less internal, but still a whole lot about those edgier emotions so prevalent in Gothic literature. Diego broods and he gets into bar fights when he's feeling some type of way. That's the type of messy self-destructive behavior that's been appealing since the early 1800s.

Female Byronic heroes are rare, but Allison fits the mold — and not just in the later seasons, where she hardens and takes some desperate measures. In the first season, Allison has the most successful and seemingly normal life out of all the siblings. Still, behind that glamorous facade, she hides her trauma and the extent of how she's used her powers. Like Cathy Earnshaw in *Wuthering Heights*, she tries to fit into a more acceptable role in society while battling who she really is and what she comes from. Another specifically female Byronic hero trait are "sad eyes" — and Emmy Raver-Lampman just has the perfect big brown eyes to convey that melancholy.

THE POWER OF THE PRETERNATURAL

All of the Hargreeves siblings have powers, but collectively, their powers are more morbid than the typical superhero, from the way they manifest to the ramifications they've had. Luther's super strength is boosted by his mutated body. Allison's reality- altering powers have destroyed her life. Even something seemingly simple like Five's portals had disastrous consequences. These powers aren't seen as boons, the way most superhero movies and shows make them out to be; they're burdens, fears manifested in a way that ties in nicely with the Gothic.

Considering how intimately his powers are tied with death, Klaus falls in line with the more traditional Gothic manifestations of ghosts and spirits. Yes, he indulges in a hedonistic lifestyle that would make Lord Byron proud, but the part of his character that really speaks to Gothic sensibilities is his supernatural ability.

He's able to communicate with ghosts and his constant companion is his dead brother Ben, whose own macabre power involved unleashing a monster inhabiting his body. In the first season, Klaus shuns his abilities for the most part, but when he's actually compelled to use them, he struggles, and the result is particularly heartbreaking.

Supernatural elements in Gothic literature (often referred to as the "preternatural," which in the 1800s had more associations with demons, witchcraft, and general trickery) were used to explore fear of the unknown. At the time of *Frankenstein,* for instance, rapid growth in science and technology challenged existing norms. Edgar Allen Poe's use of the preternatural sought to confront his own fears of madness and death. These more nebulous fears manifest as thumping hearts beneath floorboards and monsters made of body parts.

Klaus's powers challenge emotional relationships and the ideas of love and grief — themes that many superhero stories gloss over. None of the Hargreeves siblings are grieving in a healthy way; nor do any of them have a good grasp of what a normal familial relationship should look like. Klaus's connection to the dead, particularly to Ben, puts that at the forefront. The ghosts are a tangible reminder of those greater themes, while also tickling that sense of eeriness that makes Gothic and horror stories so compelling.

AN OUTCAST TO ROOT FOR

None of the Hargreeves siblings *quite* fit the role of innocent ingénue, corrupted by a dominating presence. But Viktor comes close — at least initially. What Viktor does share with the innocent ingénue is that he's initially posited as the most sympathetic to the audience, and therefore the best audience surrogate. Through his eyes, the audience learns about the family dynamics and Viktor's own suppressed powers.

But the corruptible ingénue is typically more representative of the moral good and the status quo. Viktor has far more in common with the more fringe outcasts of Gothic literature; and he shares the most with Jane Eyre, a character who on first glance appears to fit the fainting maiden archetype, but really is more shaped by ostracization than innocence. He's still someone the audience wants to root for, but not because he's the moral good. Instead, that sense of isolation turns him into a sympathetic character, an underdog to root for, but also one that some might find themselves connecting with.

By the nature of being superpowered and adopted by Reginald Hargreeves, all of the main cast are outcasts to society, but Viktor exemplifies the trope the best. He is an outcast among outcasts, kept separate from his siblings for most of their childhood because he didn't exhibit any powers.

His isolation fuels most of the first season. Even though Reginald's death brings the siblings together, Viktor still struggles to connect with the rest of them. Though their shared childhoods were all awful, Viktor's was a particular nightmare, wandering the halls of the academy, never quite sure if his siblings accept him, or if he will ever belong.

His two-fold ostracization — from greater society for being a Hargreeves, from the Hargreeves for being "normal" — makes it so we never doubt that he would turn to the first person to give him validation, which is exactly what kicks off the end of the world. Viktor's character arc dynamically changes from his first introduction, but even in later seasons, the thread of one of the Hargreeves being more separated and isolated from the rest continues. There must always be an outcast; and more often than not, that outcast is responsible for the end of the world.

A HARBINGER OF DOOM

With his intelligence, arrogance, and cynicism, Five also checks off a number of boxes for quintessential Byronic heroes. But he has a far greater burden to bear when it comes to *The Umbrella Academy*'s Gothic elements. He's the one who's seen the end of the world, and thus he bears the prophecy that haunts them all.

Curses, omens, and prophecies are a big element of Gothic literature, which more often than not has a tragic end. With the doomed ending hanging over the narrative, the characters' actions are futile, contributing to a general sense of dread. Five has seen the future, and he's effectively a harbinger of the end of the world.

And what makes the first season of *The Umbrella Academy* so Gothic is that despite everyone's best efforts and Five's repeated warnings, everything they've been avoiding still transpires. The Hargreeves indulge in their worst impulses in order to save the world, spurning Viktor and following in their father's footsteps, and in doing so end up enabling the very thing they sought to prevent. It's a thread that continues throughout the subsequent seasons, where the siblings are trapped in a cycle of their own making, continually dooming the world.

When prophecies are fulfilled in Gothic literature, it usually signifies the end of wrongdoings. The perpetrator has been felled; whatever has plagued the castle or the family can rest. But because the Hargreeves continually evade the consequences of their own actions, they keep making similar mistakes. It's a deliciously compelling tragedy, one that plays over and over again.

THE ENDURING ALLURE OF THE GOTHIC

In the 1800s, Gothic literature sought to confront societal fears head-on. Nowadays, the landscape of continuous superhero stories rarely interrogates the more macabre and melancholy side of the genre. *The Umbrella Academy*, however, embraces all of the darker sensibilities, from the physical aesthetic to the character archetypes that turn expectations around.

There's a whole cast of characters in touch with their more disastrous emotions; a connection to the supernatural that veers more grotesque than wondrous; a setting that is as haunting as it is beautiful; and the constant reminder that doom is just around the corner. And yes, some of these elements are appealing just for entertainment

THE PSYCHGEIST OF POP CULTURE

value. A tortured antihero stalking around a gloomy mansion will always attract a certain demographic.

But at the same time, tragedy can be cathartic.

The Hargreeves siblings don't really save the day, so much as they cause the destruction of the world over and over again, narrowly evading it time and time again. There might be brooding heroes in other superhero stories, but few of them are messing up as much as these six siblings. Watching characters confront their ruinous emotions and tangle up their tense relationships, all as the world crumbles around them has a certain intoxicating intrigue. It's just as alluring to us as it was to people in the 1800s. This time, though, there's a little more iconic needle drops, time travel, and talking monkeys along the way.

NOTES

1. Neese, J., Neese, J., Blackman, S., King, J., Goldberg, K., & Richardson, M. (Executive Producers). (2019). Season 1. In *The Umbrella Academy*. Netflix.

2. Bronte, E. (2012). Wuthering Heights. Penguin Classics

3. Bronte, E. (1999). Jane Eyre. Peterborough, Ont: Broadview Press.

4. Walpole, H. (2014) The Castle of Otranto (N. Groom, Ed.; 3rd ed.). Oxford University Press

5. Radcliffe, A. (2009). The romance of the Forest (C. Chard, Ed.). Oxford University Press.

6. Cutts, D., Dodson, B., & Poe, E. A. (1982). *Edgar Allan Poe's The fall of the House of Usher*. Mahwah, N.J., Troll Associates

7. Stein, A. (2004). *The Byronic hero in film, fiction, and television*. SIU Press.

EGAD, A TALKING CHIMPANZEE!

JENNIFER FULLER, PHD

P*ogo and the Rise of the Ape Man in Popular Culture*

HAVE you ever heard the joke about the two muffins? You see, there were once these two muffins in an oven. The one muffin looks over at the other and says, "Man, it's hot in here." The other muffin replies, "Egad! A talking muffin." To be fair, I didn't say it was a *good* joke. But I bring it up because it illustrates a rather interesting cultural phenomenon – that we often accept a ridiculous premise simply because of its context. One certainly wouldn't usually expect to converse with a blueberry pastry, but as this is a joke, you don't even hesitate to accept that a baked good could speak. (See also Marlin's famous sea cucumber joke in *Finding Nemo*). Yet stopping to ask why we make such assumptions, especially in light of particular contexts, can lead us to interesting revelations about cultural history, the nature of popular media, and ourselves.

In 2019, Netflix released its adaptation of Gerard Way and

Gabriel Bá's comic, *The Umbrella Academy*[1]. At first glance, the narrative seems to be a typical science fiction adaptation, after all the source material is original and the events take place in broadly contemporary times (the futuristic present, the post- apocalyptic future, and the 1960s). Yet while the series is modern, it features two primary characters who are clear adaptations of key tropes not of contemporary cinema, but of nineteenth- century adventure fiction – our muffins if you will. The first is the academy's enigmatic founder, Sir Reginald Hargreeves, a.k.a. The Monocle. An allusion to the scientist/adventurer in works like those of H.G. Wells and Jules Verne, Hargreeves and his Indian assistant, Abhijat (who does not appear in the Netflix series) adopt and train the superhero children who form the Umbrella Academy. However, this chapter is far more interested in the enigmatic second muffin, Dr. Pogo, a chimpanzee who wears human clothing, speaks (in a British accent in the television series), and provides sage advice and emotional support to the human superheroes.

What gives Pogo his muffin status, especially in the television series which works to provide background stories for almost all the characters in the comic (even the minor ones), is that readers and viewers are asked to accept a talking chimpanzee that has found work in a contemporary superhero academy, and also somehow managed to gain an advanced degree, without any explanatory material. When the show debuted, not a single review I could find made any mention of the oddness of a *talking chimpanzee with a British accent* being a central character. In other words, by the early 21st century, the character of the ape-man is so universally understood as a trope in cinematic adaptation that it needs no introduction. But how did this trope come to be so established in our minds that we never think to ask about the "talking muffin", how it has evolved, if you can forgive an inevitable pun, from its nineteenth-century origins into its current form, and what does tracing that journey reveal about the way we understand race, gender, and humanity in popular media?

Of course, any discussion of an ape-man immediately brings to mind Charles Darwin and his role in the literary imagination of the Victorian era. Darwin's *Origin of the Species*[2] (originally published in 1859) was not only extraordinary for the scientific theory it outlined but also as it ignited speculation about how the theory could be applied to humanity (a connection Darwin had carefully tried to prevent). While the idea of the ape as a stand-in for human behavior can be traced back to the Classical era, the idea of "the missing link" or apes which could pass as humans through the marvels of evolution multiplied in nineteenth- century science writing, with clear moral and racial overtones. Apes were not just satirizing humanity by showing us the animal behaviors hidden beneath polite society (like the Yahoos in *Gulliver's Travels*[3]), they were being used to divide groups of humans and categorize them on an evolutionary hierarchy based on perceived similarities to their simian ancestors (had Pogo entered one of these lectures, he would have caused a scientific riot and years of speculation in the top journals). But while mid- nineteenth century scientists raised questions around human behavior and classification, as Bernard Lightman has noted, "It wasn't until the 1880s that a large number of popularizers of science began to convey evolution to the Victorian reading audience in children's literature, in biographies of Darwin, and in sweeping histories of the development of life on earth. Many of the best-selling books popularizing evolution did not appear until the 1890s."[4] In the history of literature, that's surprisingly recent.

Scientific theories aren't usually of great interest to the general reading public unless they connect with ideas of progress or fears of social decline. Mass media explanations of human evolution and ideas of an actual ape-man hybrid dovetailed nicely with emerging fears of waning political power and physical and moral degeneracy that began to haunt the European literary imagination at the end of the century. After all, England wasn't the superpower she had once been and the looming threat of war, and who would be best poised to win it, were subjects of everyday conversation. The average person, not just the scientific elite, began to ask where the lines were between primitive peoples and apes. Was it possible apes were not simply being mistaken for humans, as in Poe's "Murders in the Rue Morgue"[5] (originally published in 1841), but that they could be indistinguishable from them as the boundaries between man, monster, and beast began to blur under these new ideas? The age was ripe for a new type of fictional trope.

WHAT MAKES A MONKEY AND WHAT MAKES A MAN? QUESTIONING HUMANITY IN *THE MYSTERIOUS ISLAND*

Jules Verne, the inventor of "speculative" scientific fiction, leaped at the chance to exploit the blurred lines between ape and man in *The Mysterious Island*[6] (originally published in 1875). The novel is a fairly typical example of late-nineteenth-century shipwreck fiction featuring an engineer and his fellow castaways recreating civilization on a remote island in the Pacific to explain scientific processes to the reading audience – as one does in these sorts of books. But the novel also demonstrates how the figure of the ape-man had become a racially loaded stereotype. The explorers discover one of these new creatures when it invades Granite Cave, their island home, and the friendly but lower-class (and thus often silly) sailor Pencroff remarks, "It's a monkey, a macaque, a capuchin, a guenon, an orangutan, a baboon, a gorilla, a marmoset! Our home has been invaded by monkeys!"[7] Funny, yes, but Verne's exhaustive list of primates is not simply for comic effect. He wants to emphasize this particular ape's curious appearance as "it was a tall ape, unmistakably of the primate order–of that there was no doubt. Whether chimpanzee, orangutan, gorilla, or gibbon, it could clearly be classified among the anthropomorphs, so named for their resemblance to the human race."[8] Visually, there is quite a difference between the gorilla and the orangutan as even an untrained eye can tell you, but for Verne, this animal's resemblance to humanity makes its species indistinct – it's something new.

Paradoxically, in attempting to use science to view the ape as an impartial scientific subject, Verne makes the ape racially and socially charged. After the castaways capture their specimen, Harbert suggests that the ape, which Pencroff refers to as a "blackamoor," should be made their servant. As Verne writes, "[The ape's] facial angle was not perceptibly inferior to that of an Australian or Hottentot, which confirmed his place in the ranks of the anthropomorphs. . . . Put to work in houses, they can serve at table, clean the rooms, care for the laundry, wax shoes, skillfully use a knife, fork, and spoon, even drink wine. . . much like any other bipedal, featherless domestic"[9] While Verne seeks to view the animal from the position of objective scientific observer, his language is loaded with racist and classist overtones. While literary critics have often seen Verne as a simple recorder of scientific progress (often to the detriment of plot and character), his choices reveal his slippage between dispassionate scientific observation and the nineteenth-century racial and cultural hierarchy ingrained in his assumptions. In this passage, Verne demonstrates how the ape works as a stand-in both for "unevolved" cultures but also social classes. Verne makes the ape a perfect servant: silent, efficient, and simple.

The novel doubles down on this idea of the ape as a type of lesser human through Verne's comparisons between him and the recently freed domestic slave, Neb. One reason Verne includes Americans in the novel is to celebrate the North's victory in the Civil War and show his support for abolitionists, but while Verne despised the institution of slavery, he struggled with portraying Neb as an individual with wants and desires equal to those of the white characters. The main protagonist, Cyrus Smith, "had given the Negro his liberty many years before, but the liberated slave refused to leave his master's side."[10] Upon finding the ape, Pencroff is quick to reassure Ned, that he does not need to be jealous. Master Joop, as the ape is named, will prove a superior servant as "he doesn't quibble over the wages!"[11] Even while Verne championed ideas of freedom and liberty, he saw little distinction between Ned and Joop who both made excellent and loyal unpaid workers. Highly intelligent, Joop is quickly "elevated to the position of manservant," wearing clothing and posing in human attitudes.[12] Much of the animal's elevated status comes from Ned who "had taken great pains to train the nimble orangutan in his daily task, and the Negro and the ape genuinely seemed to understand each other when they spoke."[13] The comic nature of such scenes indicates that Verne means to flatter Joop rather than insult Ned, but it is clear that late nineteenth-century ideas about the racial hierarchy of mankind have permeated the character of the ape-man. As Bill Ashcroft explains, "What may seem on the surface an attempt at re-thinking the status of the animal is in fact a confirmation of the racial hierarchy established by imperial rule. The novel is unable to negotiate the contradictions of the ape's position because the imperative of racial hierarchy in the colonising project is so strong."[14] Even an author sympathetic to the cause of finding equality among mankind seems unable to break free from the stereotype that some humans are closer to their Darwinian ancestor, and thus have kinship with advanced apes.

ADAPTING THE APE-MAN: CINEMATIC VISIONS OF *DR JEKYLL AND MR HYDE*

While Verne is looking specifically at an ape who can function as a human, in other literary works it was media adaptation rather than the fiction itself which caused readers to connect characters with creatures. In these adapted works, we can see hints of how a very early version of Pogo developed. In the *Strange Case of Dr Jekyll and Mr Hyde* (1886), Robert Louis Stevenson leaves it to the reader to connect his villain with ideas of the beast-man. While many modern readers have envisioned the villainous Mr Hyde as having simian characteristics, Stevenson's depiction in the novella is intentionally vague. Hyde is described by observers at the first encounter as a "damned Juggernaut" but still a man, though one with "a kind of black, sneering coolness–frightened too, I could see that–but carrying it off, sir, really like Satan."[15] When pressed, one of the narrators explains, "He is not easy to describe. There is something wrong with his appearance; something displeasing, something downright detestable . . . He must be deformed somewhere; he gives off a strong feeling of deformity . . . He's an extraordinary looking man, and yet I really can name nothing out of the way."[16] While this idea of deformity and evil continues in descriptions of Hyde, nothing in the text refers to him as animal-like or specifically ape-like, with one notable exception. When Hyde commits an unprovoked attack on Sir Danvers Carew, a wealthy elderly gentleman, he is described as clubbing him with "ape-like fury"[17] and at the end of the text Jekyll writes that he fears "the action of [Hyde's] apelike spite."[18] Both quotes reference Hyde's attitude, his inability to control emotion, not his physical appearance.

Our notion of Hyde appearing as an ape-man thus comes not from Stevenson's manuscript but from the various popular adaptations of the text. The 1912 film adaptation depicted Hyde as impish and fanged, though still distinctly human. However, it was the 1920s adaptation that gave Hyde a more bestial form, with John Barrymore adding hairy ape-like hands to the fangs and wide eyes portrayed in the earlier film. The 1931 adaptation embraces a highly ape-like Hyde, with dark skin and pronounced canines, similar to portrayals in illustrations and comics. The idea of the twin personalities in the book had moved the director to not simply depict the ordinary Jekyll and the evil Hyde but instead embrace the idea of Hyde's evil as connected to ideas of the unevolved monster, the ape-man.

The idea of Hyde as an ape is embedded in our contemporary imagination as we can see from Alan Moore and Kevin O Neill's rendering of Hyde in their reimagination of nineteenth-century adventure heroes in their comic book series *The League of Extraordinary Gentlemen* (1999-2019). Hyde is depicted as twice the size of the average man and gorilla-like in attributes, often shirtless to show his overtly muscular physique (in many ways similar to portrayals of Marvel's The Incredible Hulk). His form is depicted as more ape than man, and he is shown breaking limbs and ripping flesh with his fangs. He also has much darker skin and heavier features than the pasty, thin Jekyll and is covered in a fine layer of hair. This Hyde's monstrosity is connected to both his immense strength and his barbarousness, being useful to the team of gentlemen with his ability to kill without mercy or remorse.

Yet how did the idea of evil and deformity come to be translated into the idea of Hyde as an ape-man? It was you, consumer of media! Audiences have participated in the act of adaption, translating Hyde's deformity through a Darwinian lens. At several points in the novella, Stevenson gestures to the idea of Hyde as somehow inhuman or less evolved. As one character describes Hyde, "The man seems hardly human! Something troglodytic, shall we say? . . . Or is it the mere radiance of a foul soul that thus transpires through, and transfigures, its clay continent? . . .if ever I read Satan's signature upon a face, it is on that of your new friend."[19] The use of "troglodytic" here references the most common nineteenth-century usage, describing Hyde as prehistoric, with a sense of the secluded hermit (while "troglodyte" was used to refer to anthropoid apes in scientific literature beginning in the eighteenth century, the Victorian use of the adjective form refers to primitive humans[20]). Most readers understandably confuse the term with the scientific usage of the noun "troglodyte" which can include anthropoid apes. Other details seized on by adaptors include one transformation of Hyde where "his face became suddenly black" and another where Hyde's hand appears "lean, corded, knuckly, of a dusky pallor and thickly shaded with a swart growth of hair."[21] It makes sense that when directors desperate to please audiences begging for visual media began looking for a way to depict Hyde's unnaturalness, they often decided to combine these physical descriptors (primitive, darker skin, hairy body) with Stevenson's "ape-like fury" and portrayed Hyde as having simian features.

Yet this choice to represent Hyde as less than human comes with some problematic baggage. As the 1931 adaptation shows, it was easy to infuse the ape-like Hyde with racial stereotypes of African Americans in cinema. Stevenson's pairing of Hyde's evil with a sense of deformity lends itself to each generation's idea of how to visualize the "wrong" or "unnatural." Often this leads to depictions of Hyde mapped through stereotypes of race as well as gender—as we see in Alan Moore's adaptation, Hyde is often depicted as masculinity unleashed from social constraint, as uninhibited testosterone. For readers, Hyde's moral degeneration is often mapped onto what our subconscious sees as monstrous, and thus adaptations help reveal how each era reframes and recontextualizes the idea of evil in society. The lingering power of Hyde to appear in our mind's eye as an ape even into the modern age reveals that, like those Victorian novelists, we still fear our inner animal and wonder if the deviant among us, the serial killers and the rapists, are somehow mirrors into our less-evolved impulses.

ARE WE NOT MEN? EVOLVING THE APE-MAN IN *THE ISLAND OF DOCTOR MOREAU*

While the *Strange Case of Dr Jekyll and Mr Hyde* shows how readers have often used the character of the ape-man as a way of interpreting evil, for H.G. Wells the trope moves from metaphorical to literal. In *The Island of Doctor Moreau*[22] (originally published in 1896), Wells asks readers to imagine the ape-man not as a sort of metaphor or mask for criminality and corruption, but as a biological reality. While the ape-man is often used as a way to speak about humanity (apes that act human or humans that act like apes), few authors dared to explore the idea of actually merging man and beast. For Wells, the idea of the ape-man was at the heart of the central question haunting nineteenth-century science: what actually did separate man from beast?

The question confronts Edward Prendick, the novel's protagonist, almost as soon as he is shipwrecked upon this mysterious island. Upon exploring Moreau's vivisection lab (vivisection was the dissection of live animals for scientific research), Moreau is haunted by the origins of the hybrid creatures that populate the island. His probing question, "Could the vivisection of men be possible?" points to the heart of his confusion, are these animals transformed into humans or humans grafted with animal parts? Prendick's instinct is for the latter, allowing him to link "the grotesque animalism of the islanders with his abominations," believing that Moreau must be experimenting on the less evolved races of the island.[23] Prendick's assumption hints again at one of the functions of the ape-man character, to reveal the missing link between our ancient ancestors, apes, and modern "evolved" humanity. In this hierarchy, an ape-man would be a regression of progress, cutting and transforming a "lesser" human until it resembles an ape.

However, as it is eventually revealed, Moreau's work is actually a form of progression, evolving animals into subhumans through the use of scientific experimentation. Moreau explains to Prendick that he isn't simply molding the physical structures of the animals but attempting to understand and replicate the complexity of human experience, behavior, and thought. As he notes, "Very much indeed of what we call moral education is such an artificial modification and perversion of instinct; pugnacity is trained into courageous self-sacrifice, and suppressed sexuality into religious emotion. And the greatest difference between man and monkey is in the larynx.[24]" Prendick disagrees, believing there must be a greater difference between humans and animals than simple biology and defying the idea of moral law as simply trained instinct.

The novel's ape-man sits at the crossroads of their debate, as Prendick and Moreau both seem to find him the least objectionable of the experiments. And Moreau's decision to begin his experiments creating beast-men with an ape-man is highly intentional. Moreau chose a gorilla for his first experiment, since apes are closest to the human form, and spent a week molding him, with much "added, much changed. [Moreau] thought him a fair specimen of the negroid type."[25] Moreau's greatest triumph is not simply in creating an ape that resembles a human, but in convincing others that he is one.

After teaching the creature to read and count, if slowly, Moreau introduces him to the island's inhabitants who after their initial uncertainty, accept him as a fellow human as "his ways seem so mild, and he was so abject."[26] It seems Moreau has created his own Joop, bypassing the slow process of evolution. Prendick is drawn to the ape-man for the same reason as Pencroff, his manners seem to him familiar if crude. It is the ape-man that allows him entry into the circle of beast-men and helps him to learn the Law, the set of rules the beast-men follow to behave as humans. Even the ape-man himself seems to be aware that his human-like form gives him special status, telling the other creatures "He is a five-man, a five-man, a five-man...like me," showing that he and Prendick share five digits and opposable thumbs. For the beast-men, their question is the same as Prendick and Moreau's, wondering aloud *"Are we not Men?"* at the end of each repetition of the Law.

Unlike earlier ape-men we have seen, who show the elevated state of animals or the lowered possibilities of human nature (or Victorian racial theory), Wells asks us to consider what the real difference is between human and ape-man, a term that has at its heart a basic redundancy. Montgomery (Moreau's assistant) retreats into Latin, arguing *"Hi non sunt homines, sunt animalia qui nos habemus...vivisected"* to which Prendick rebuts, "They talk, build houses, cook. They were men." (Roughly translated, "These are not people, these are animals that we have...vivisected.")[27] Readers have been operating under the assumption that Moreau has tortured the ape to transform it into a man-like creature, but Prendick begins to wonder where the line is that divides these beast-men from his own evolution. Prendick's revelation reminds contemporary readers of Jane Goodall's discovery that chimpanzees use tools, shattering ideas of the traditional boundaries between ape and man. But beyond even their mechanical skills, their use of opposable thumbs, Prendick observes, "The rest stood silent–watching. They may have once been animals. But never before did I see an animal trying to think."[28] Clearly, Prendick means a higher level of thinking, arguing that perhaps the difference between man and beast is simply a matter of what we might refer to as reason or logic, not muscles and meat, refusing to accept Montgomery's overly simplistic Latin explanation.

After asking readers to question why the ape-man is not just a new type of human, Wells quickly moves to asking why the humans are not simply beasts – a question not just biological but ethical. Montgomery's lack of religious principles and addiction to alcohol proves to have disastrous consequences in a tense moment when he attempts to share brandy with the dog-man, M'ling. Prendick is quick to resist the idea of sharing liquor with a beast, to which Montgomery retorts, "Beast!. . .You're the beast. [M'ling] takes his liquor like a Christian."[29] After Montgomery pulls his revolver, Prendick decides discretion is the better part of valor and remarks, "You've made a beast of yourself. To the beasts you may go."[30] While the ape-man and his compatriots are certainly not models of human exceptionalism, neither are the mad scientist, the drunken lout, or the cowardly explorer with whom they share the island.

By the end of the novel, both Moreau and Montgomery have been dispatched and Prendick is left alone with the rapidly degenerating beast-men. Yet Wells hints that this degeneration is not simply biological as Prendick too finds himself reverting to his more ape-like self. Prendick himself notes he "became one among the Beast People in the Island of Doctor Moreau"[31]; the ape-man is unable to distinguish himself from Prendick who notes he has "undergone strange changes. My clothes hung about me as yellow rags, through whose rents glowed the tanned skin. My hair grew long, and became matted together. I am told even now my eyes have a strange brightness, a swift alertness of movement."[32] By the time Prendick is rescued and returned to society, he is almost unable to tell human from ape-man. As he views individuals around him, he remarks, "I could not persuade myself that the men and women I met were not also another, still passably human, Beast People, animals half-wrought into the outward image of human souls; and that they would presently begin to revert, to show first this bestial mark and then that."[33] For Prendick, the ape-man may have been a creation of Moreau's lab, but he fears the ape within the man as well, worrying "I feel as though the animal was surging up through [others]; that presently the degradation of the Islanders will be played over again on a larger scale."[34] Prendick claims to resist these impulses, believing his fellow humans have overcome their baser instincts and are free from the ludicrous Law, yet Wells makes it clear that the distinction between man and ape-man is far more tenuous than we might like to believe. We may well ask of Pogo, *Is he not Man?*

WE'RE ALL A LITTLE APISH HERE: THE ROLE OF NATURE AND NURTURE IN *TARZAN OF THE APES*

If *The Island of Doctor Moreau* is primarily concerned with showing humanity's similarities to the ape-man, Edgar Rice Burroughs' *Tarzan of the Apes* has the opposite goal: to distinguish the man raised by apes from the ape-man. Burroughs' tale is perhaps the best known of the ape-man stories in popular media. The story of the baby raised by apes and navigating manhood has been made into scores of adaptations (and was the product of numerous sequels by Burroughs himself, including one where Tarzan goes to Mars). Audiences remain fascinated by Tarzan who always embodies the idea that civilization, character, and intelligence are more than simply products of the environment; that man is born more than monkey.

Burroughs knew little of Africa, he never visited the continent, and he drew his characters largely from popular fiction rather than any research (the original magazine version of the story accidentally places tigers in the African jungle). Tarzan's adopted parents are not an identified species, but rather an unspecified "great anthropoid ape."[35] While Tarzan cannot match the other apes for strength or size, Burroughs makes constant mention of his superior reason, cunning, and imagination. Unlike his ape brothers who kill with fist and fang, Tarzan fashions tools like a noose to capture his prey (and mock his opponents). Yet it isn't until Tarzan teaches himself to read, using an illustrated children's book, that he begins to understand the difference between the apes and himself. The book is an alphabet primer that begins, "A is for Archer / Who shoots with a bow. B is for Boy, / His first name is Joe."[36] It is these two primitive ideas that will differentiate Tarzan throughout the novel: Tarzan can use sophisticated weapons and Tarzan is a boy, a human child.

While the novel emphasizes Tarzan's humanity, it also tests the limits of what Tarzan will and will not do because of his ape upbringing. Tarzan displays savagery both in his hunts and in his craving for meat, as "Tarzan, more than the apes, craved and needed flesh."[37] The greatest challenge for Tarzan comes when he first meets another human (an episode that is often cut from adaptations, preferring to have his first meeting with Jane and so firmly establishing the text as a romance). This first encounter is with an African, Kulonga, which puzzles Tarzan, as "the strange creature. . .was so like him in form and yet so different in face and color. His books had portrayed the *Negro*, but how different had been the dull, dead print to this sleek thing of ebony, pulsing with life . . .Tarzan recognized him not so much the *Negro* as the *Archer* of his picture book."[38] Once again it is his superior logic that allows Tarzan to categorize ape from man, noting that even though Kulonga looks and behaves differently from him, he is still an archer and therefore a boy.

Yet, once again, the character of the ape-man is used not only to distinguish humans from animals but also to categorize humans according to Victorian principles of racial hierarchy. Burrough makes much of Kulonga's primitivism, dwelling on his tattooing, filed teeth, and feathered headdress. He also raises the question of which man, Tarzan or Kulonga, is closer to being the regressive ape-man. Tarzan's instincts are also "savage," as he ponders whether to eat the corpse of Kulonga (who he has killed to avenge his adopted ape mother), and the narrator explains, "Tarzan of the Apes was hungry, and here was meat; meat of the kill, which jungle ethics permitted him to eat. How may we judge him, by what standards, this ape-man with the heart and head and body of an English gentleman, and the training of a wild beast?"[39] The novel notes that Tarzan would never presume to eat a fellow ape but considers Kulonga simply one of the many animals of the jungle and thus fair game, in the original sense of the phrase. Tarzan, as a man raised by an ape, should have no biological reason to resist eating Kulonga. However, Tarzan hesitates, wondering if humans are allowed to eat fellow humans and becomes physically ill at the thought. While Tarzan's logic is unable to answer this important moral quandary, the narrator notes, "All [Tarzan] knew was that he could not eat the flesh of this black man, and thus hereditary instinct, ages old, usurped the functions of his untaught mind and saved him."[40]

The novel initially shows Tarzan distinguishing himself from the apes through his superior cunning and seems to argue that what separates man from ape is education, intelligence, and logic. However, Tarzan's encounter with Kulonga flips the narrative, arguing that there is an instinctive "Britishness" within Tarzan that will not allow him to regress to his primitive bestial nature. As the novel progresses, it is clear that while Burroughs refers to Tarzan as an ape-man, he is using the trope not to show a hybrid between the two, as we have seen in other texts, but a dichotomy: Tarzan is raised ape but born man, and the two are never able to live harmoniously. Tarzan's journey thus echoes ideas of popular Victorian Darwinism, that man (specifically British man) has evolved beyond his ape-man ancestors and even when removed from society, humanity is more than simply an educated aping of ideas.

UNDER HUMANITY'S UMBRELLA: MOVING BEYOND THE APE-MAN

And after this wandering journey, we find ourselves back to considering *Umbrella Academy's* Pogo and what reflections he offers on how the ape-man character is still relevant in our cultural canon. As I mentioned early on, one of the most intriguing aspects of *The Umbrella Academy* is that it makes no attempt in the first season to explain why one of the central characters is a talking chimpanzee. Instead, the show draws on the extensive audience knowledge of popular portrayals of ape- man characters, such as those I have discussed, to fill in the missing storyline. By merely hinting that Sir Reginald Hargreeves is a Victorian adventure hero and eccentric and referencing his work on "the cerebral enhancement of the chimpanzee," the comic establishes a world where all the characters find it perfectly ordinary to have an ape-man as the house butler (and physician). Intriguingly, the television adaptation drops even the brief reference to Hargreeves' work on apes as well as the comic's only explanatory illustration, where one of the characters has a vision of Pogo drawn in sickly green, caged and hooked up to vivid red wires and sensors, with a central image of his eyes forced open and dilated. The character, Number Five, exclaims "My god Pogo! The lab! I never knew–!" before fainting in psychic pain.[41]

Instead of commenting on race relations or focusing on scientific experimentation, both the comic and the television adaptation focus on Pogo's role in the dysfunctional family of superheroes. Pogo is not an object of pity (for the characters or the audience) and nor is he seen as in any way different from the humans—no one in the show ever remarks on his simian status. Pogo is offered as a foil to the emotional cruelty of Sir Hargreeves, the children's adopted father, who presumably sees them only as tools for saving humanity. It is Pogo who offers the listening ear and comforts the children in times of emotional distress. In one of the kindest scenes in the drama, he reassures Vanya (Number Seven, Elliot Page) that they are a member of the family and that they are special, even if they believe they have no powers. He also provides the requisite DNA to repair Luther (Number One, Tom Hopper) after he is horribly injured in a botched mission.

It is Luther who fulfills the more traditional role of the ape- man in both the series and the comic, though he mostly works to question ideas of masculinity. Luther is physically strong but emotionally unevolved – the television adaptation includes scenes that mock his lack of sexual experience and his inability to lead the others (the way Hargreeves presumably intended). Luther, like many of the other superheroes, rejects his powers, especially since his ape-enhanced body makes him appear unnatural (particularly to women). The show and the comic move away from using ape-man's traditional role to provide commentary on race. All of the children are portrayed as white in the comic, but the Netflix adaptation includes a racially diverse cast. Luther is played by a white actor, but in neither the comic nor the adaptation is Luther's ape form a visual reference point to black individuals, consciously avoiding the racial stereotypes that plagued earlier illustrations of the ape-man. Gerard Way's concept art shows Luther in shades of sky blue and vivid green (rather than the traditional black or brown tones) and the Netflix adaptation matches Luther's prosthetics to the actor's natural skin tone and hair color. Both the comic and the television show leave Luther's face unchanged.

If Luther is the more traditional ape-man of the series, then it stands to reason that Pogo serves a different purpose. He does not provide the expected commentary on race or gender, nor does he raise any questions about which species is genetically or intellectually superior. Instead, Pogo asks readers and viewers to examine our ideas about human's assumed emotional superiority. He is the only truly compassionate character in the comic (and arguably the show), and also the most mature, handling crises with tact and honesty (even if he doesn't always make the right choices). *The Umbrella Academy* shows that the ape-man, or man-ape, still serves as a mirror to our understanding of humanity and our place in the hierarchy of animals. Yet while Victorians may have used the character to assert principles of racial or gender superiority, this modern adaptation instead uses the trope to investigate emotional superiority. According to *The Umbrella Academy*, humanity must master compassion, kindness, and empathy before we can imagine ourselves as evolved as our favorite humble chimpanzee. Perhaps we should all spend a bit more time listening for the talking muffins.

NOTES

1. Way, Gerard and Gabriel Bá. *The Umbrella Academy: Apocalypse Suite.* Milwaukie: Dark Horse Books, 2008.
2. *Darwin, Charles, 1809-1882. (1859). On the origin of species by means of natural selection, or preservation of favoured races in the struggle for life. London :John Murray*
3. Swift, J. (1985). *Gulliver's travels.* New York, Avenel Books.
4. Bernard Lightman, "The Popularization of Evolution and Victorian Culture," in *Evolution and Victorian Culture*, ed. Bernard Lightman and Bennett Zon (Cambridge: Cambridge University Press, 2014), 288.
5. Poe, E.A. (2009). The murders in the rue morgue. Vintage Classics.
6. Verne, J. (2008). The Mysterious Island. Project Gutemberg, ebook 1268
7. Jules Verne, *The Mysterious Island*, ed. Jordan Stump, trans. Caleb Carr, (New York: Modern Library, 2004), 315.
8. Verne, *Mysterious Island, p.* 315.
9. Verne, *Mysterious Island,* p. 319.
10. Verne, *Mysterious Island,* p. 15.
11. Verne, *Mysterious Island,* p. 321.
12. Verne, *Mysterious Island, p.* 339.
13. Verne, *Mysterious Island, p.* 339.
14. Bill Ashcroft, "Colonisation and Specisism: Jules Verne's *The Mysterious Island,*" *Kunapipi* 34, no. 2 (2012): 150.
15. Robert Louis Stevenson, *Strange Case of Dr Jekyll and Mr Hyde and Other Tales*, ed. Roger Luckhurst (Oxford: Oxford University Press, 2006), 7.

16. Stevenson, *Strange Case*, p. 9.
17. Stevenson, *Strange Case*, p. 20.
18. Stevenson, *Strange Case*, p. 66.
19. Stevenson, *Strange Case*, p. 16.
20. Stevenson, R. L. (2006). *Strange Case of Dr Jekyll and Mr Hyde and Other Tales*. Edited by Roger Luckhurst. Oxford: Oxford University Press, N. 16.
21. Stevenson, *Strange Case*, p. 58.
22. Wells, H. G. (2005). The Island of Doctor Moreau. London: Penguin.
23. Wells, *The Island*, p. 52.
24. Wells, *The Island*, p. 73.
25. Wells, *The Island*, p. 76.
26. Wells, *The Island*, p. 76.
27. Wells, *The Island*, p. 67.
28. Wells, *The Island*, p. 69.
29. Wells, *The Island*, p. 107.
30. Wells, *The Island*, p. 107.
31. Wells, *The Island*, p. 118.
32. Wells, *The Island*, p. 124.
33. Wells, *The Island*, p. 130.
34. Wells, *The Island*, p. 130.
35. Edgar Rice Burroughs, *Tarzan of the Apes* (New York: Modern Library, 2003), 25.
36. Burroughs, *Tarzan, p.* 47.
37. Burroughs, *Tarzan, p.* 60.
38. Burroughs, *Tarzan, p.* 74. Emphasis original.
39. Burroughs, *Tarzan, p.* 78.
40. Burroughs, *Tarzan, p.* 78.
41. Way and Bá, *The Umbrella Academy*. Chapter Five.

IT'S NOT ME, IT'S YOU: CHILDHOOD TRAUMA'S IMPACT ON ADULT SIBLING RELATIONSHIPS

JASMINE HEYWARD

T elevision can be a powerful tool for changing how people think about mental illness[1] as it creates an opportunity to explore complex psychological phenomena in a way that is interesting and understandable even for those with no formal training in psychology. The connections we make with the fictional characters we see on the screen, which researchers call "parasocial relationships," can shape our thinking, the same way that forming relationships with people different than us can change our views[2]. We feel we know these characters, and maybe we can relate to them, even though we do not know them at all. (Heck, they aren't even real people!).

Though the upcoming apocalypse is the primary plot point of the first season of *The Umbrella Academy*, many of its conflicts are driven by the Hargreeves siblings' trauma, maladaptive coping mechanisms, and resentments of each other. Not only does this make for a particularly captivating television drama, but it also provides a compelling framework for examining how childhood trauma can impact adult sibling relationships. In this chapter, we are going to explore just that.

The chapter will open with a brief exploration of complex trauma, attachment, and sibling relationship dynamics to set the foundation of understanding how the Hargreeves' siblings childhood experiences connect to their adult behavior patterns. Then, we will use that information to explore how the siblings play distinct roles in the family dynamic — enforcers (Luther and Allison), rebels (Diego and Five), and absentees (Klaus and Viktor).

After establishing these roles, we will explore how the siblings justify their maladaptive coping mechanisms through comparisons to the other siblings' behavior. Detailed analysis of the relationships between Luther and Diego, Luther and Klaus, and Diego and Klaus will be used to demonstrate how each of the siblings initially believed their role to be superior and how shifts in their relationships on-screen may provide insight into conversations and interventions that can help siblings begin to heal their adult relationships.

AN INTRODUCTION TO COMPLEX TRAUMA

Alongside the recognized symptoms of trauma and post- traumatic stress disorder (PTSD), researchers and clinicians have identified a second group of symptoms that can occur among people who have experienced multiple prolonged or extended traumas over time[3]. This phenomenon is often referred to as "complex trauma" (2020) and it most commonly occurs in contexts in which someone is repeatedly traumatized in an environment that is difficult or impossible to escape[4]. Common symptoms of complex trauma include difficulty maintaining relationships, an unstable sense of self, and dysfunctional behavior[5,6] . Many also struggle to manage and process strong emotions ("emotional dysregulation" or "affect dysregulation"), leading to impulsive behavior and difficulties getting out of unpleasant mood states[7,8].

These symptoms are apparent in many of the unhealthy traits and behaviors demonstrated by the Hargreeves siblings in season one, including shallow or non-existent personal relationships, identities based on what the siblings do rather than who they are, and maladaptive responses to stress including violence, substance use, and manipulation. Considering that the siblings were raised in a highly traumatizing and dysfunctional home, understanding complex trauma and its impacts can provide a helpful framework for analyzing the siblings' interactions with each other.Defining Complex Trauma-Related Disorders

While exact diagnostic criteria for PTSD vary slightly, it is generally associated with three symptom clusters: re- experiencing the traumatic event in the present, deliberate avoidance of reminders of the event, and persistent perceptions of heightened threat[9]. For a diagnosis of PTSD, someone must have experienced a trauma that has resulted in symptoms in each of the three categories, resulting in notable difficulties functioning in day-to-day life.

There is not a clear consensus on the best way to label, diagnose, and describe the seemingly different collection of symptoms associated with complex trauma[10]. Some believe that there should be a separate name to describe these common symptoms, arguing that a separate diagnosis could help people find and access care designed for their specific experiences[11]. Others think that adding a separate diagnosis for a disorder that is similar to the already well-known PTSD would just cause confusion[12]. There are a few common proposals among those who support a separate diagnosis.

Complex Post-traumatic Stress Disorder (CPTSD) was recently added to the 11th edition of the International Classification of Diseases (ICD-11)[13]. ICD-11 is a global reference manual that defines all types of illness, disability, and medical concerns. In the newest release, CPTSD is defined as a "disorder specifically associated with stress" (2023) that is distinct from PTSD[14]. Along with the symptoms above, an ICD-11 CPTSD diagnosis also requires difficulties with affect regulation, negative self-concept associated with guilt or shame, and difficulties sustaining relationships.

There is a significant overlap between CPTSD and the proposed

Developmental Trauma Disorder (DTD), which targets children and adolescents who have experienced complex traumas impacting their development[15]. The key difference between this and CPTSD is that the DTD criteria address how developmental trauma can impact young people's cognition (i.e., thoughts) and executive functioning (i.e., a range of behaviors and skills we use to coordinate our lives, such as planning ahead and self-control). A DTD diagnosis would require impairments in "sustained attention, learning, or coping with stress," (2009, p. 6) acknowledging how childhood or adolescent complex trauma can result in symptoms that appear like ADHD, developmental disorders, or learning disabilities[16].

These symptom clusters provide additional context for the underlying causes of the challenging interpersonal dynamics between the Hargreaves siblings.

ATTACHMENT STYLES AND RELATIONSHIP DYSFUNCTION

Alongside the impacts on one's thoughts and executive functioning experiencing complex trauma can also result in long-term relationship dysfunction due to insecure attachment. Attachment theory is a psychological theory that explains the emotional bonds and social relationships between people. According to this theory, it is essential for people to have confidence that they are competent and lovable and that others will respond to and be supportive of their needs[17]. When this happens, it you form what is called a "secure attachment". When children's needs are unmet, they often develop one of several styles of insecure attachment, which results in relationship habits that are designed to help a child avoid emotional or physical harm. These habits, however, become destructive in the long run.

In the Hargreeves siblings' case, their father was often distant and, at times, cruel, and their mother's affections were tainted because she was a synthetic invention of their father's created solely so he could avoid parental duties. Sir Hargreeves routinely ignored his children's questions, concerns, and affection, encouraged conflict between the siblings, forced them into unsafe situations, and isolated them from the world outside of missions. Amongst the siblings, all three types of insecure attachment (described below) are present.

Viktor's preoccupied or anxious-ambivalent attachment is a major plot point in the first season[18]. He has thoroughly internalized the idea that he has nothing valuable to contribute and will never be the best at anything, and he is therefore unlikely to form relationships in which people will reliably support him. When he meets "Leonard", who seems to be an exception, Viktor quickly becomes overinvested in that relationship, due to a combination of being disproportionately grateful for Leonard's attention and an intense fear of abandonment. In episode four, when Allison says she feels something is off about him, Viktor perceives it as an attempt to cut him off from the only person who makes him feel happy and special[19]. His desperate need for external validation is largely why Leonard (aka Harold Jenkins) can isolate and manipulate him so thoroughly.

Luther, Klaus, and Five all display anxious-avoidant attachment, meaning they have little desire for deep and intimate relationships and struggle to express emotions in front of others[20]. Most common amongst people who were punished for expressing emotion by caregivers and/or peers, they have learned to keep up a strong facade regardless of the environment and rely on themselves over others. This style can also be associated with arrogance and a sense that these people are stronger and more competent than the others around them, which is certainly on display with Luther and Five[21]. In other cases, the facade does not project strength or self-sufficiency, yet it still relies on emotional dishonesty and avoidance. This avoidance prevents more meaningful connections with their siblings.

Finally, Diego and Allison display disorganized or fearful-avoidant attachment. While they are interested in meaningful relationships, they tend to self-sabotage because they are simultaneously terrified of vulnerability[22]. They will avoid the hard and potentially distressing parts of relationships at all costs, likely harming their loved ones in the process. When Detective Patch brings up his relationship with his past, Diego stonewalls her to prevent a meaningful conversation[23]. Allison, on the other hand, uses her compulsion power on her daughter to avoid the feeling of helplessness that comes with having no idea how to address her daughter's distress. Disorganized attachment in childhood tends to develop into one of two behavior patterns: hostile and conflict-seeking or nice-seeming but emotionally manipulative[24]. In season one, Diego is the former and Allison is the latter.

The interplay of these different insecure attachment styles is an additional factor in the level of conflict among the siblings.

COLLECTIVE TRAUMA IN SIBLING RELATIONSHIPS

Among the more general implications of complex trauma and insecure attachment, there are specific dynamics that appear in sibling relationships. Sibling comparison processes play a key role in development, and in the case of dysfunctional families, they can also be a major source of conflict and trauma[25].

In most cases, children will choose to be different from their siblings in interests and personal qualities to create a unique identity[26]. This tendency, known as sibling deidentification, protects siblings from social comparison that can lead to rivalry, envy, and resentment. If two siblings choose to specialize in the same thing, one is likely to be superior and the other inferior, leading to a competitive and potentially hostile dynamic[27].

Sir Hargreeves actively prevents sibling deidentification among his children as he puts them all through the same training emphasizing the same shared purpose of saving the world. It is not coincidental that Luther and Diego appear to have the most openly hostile relationship — they are the two that were most directly competing throughout their childhood and adolescence. As combat specialists, one of them was always bound to be superior, and this was arguably predetermined by the numbers given to them by their father. Luther is Number One: the leader, and Diego is Number Two: talented and essential to the team but never the best.

In Season One: *Man on the Moon*, Luther reveals that he is still emotionally invested in this at least a decade later, and he projects this onto Diego[28]. He assumes that Diego moved out at seventeen because he could not handle the idea of Luther being superior; Diego counters that he moved out because he wanted to figure out who he was outside the family as most teenagers do at that age. Both these ideas tie to deidentification, but Luther's assertion speaks to envy and rivalry while Diego's rationale highlights how the prevention of sibling deidentification led to a feeling of enmeshment. The siblings were so tied to the family identity and their shared cause that their only well-defined individual traits were their numbers and varied powers.

Another factor is differential treatment from caregivers. Children who believe their parents have favorites are more likely to have behavioral issues and troubled relationships with their parents[29]. In adult siblings, parental differential treatment is also correlated with depression and psychological distress[30]. Sir Hargreeves' deeply conditional affection led to different siblings having wildly different experiences with him. He seemingly valued competence and obedience, and those who struggled with things he valued or refused to toe the line were treated harshly.

SIBLING ROLES IN THE FAMILY

Taking into consideration the interactions between complex trauma, attachment, and the nature of sibling relationships, we can begin to explore the habits and coping mechanisms of the Hargreeves siblings — from the perspective of their roles in the family system and their responses to trauma.

REVIEW OF FAMILY-ROLE AND TRAUMA-RESPONSE TYPOLOGIES

Over the past seventy-five years, both researchers and mental health clinicians have defined classification systems to describe the roles that children play in dysfunctional families and the behavioral responses they may have.

Possibly the most well-known system for trauma responses is the four Fs: fight, flight, fawn, and freeze31:

- The fight response seeks to establish power and control through intimidation as this is expected to protect the person responding.
- The flight response focuses on simply avoiding threats and uncomfortable emotions, either through leaving an environment or through checking out mentally and emotionally.
- Freezing leads to self-isolation and dissociation as a self-protection strategy.
- Fawning seeks to get on an abuser or authority figure's good side by making concessions even if they violate the respondent's dignity, autonomy, or safety.

Many people with CPTSD present with more than one of these responses regularly, leading to the creation of more complex roles.

Therapists have also identified common responses among their clients who experienced significant trauma in their families. One example is "rebel, join, or freeze"[32]. While the system was initially designed to represent childhood behavior, there are implications for adolescence and adulthood.

- Children and teenagers who rebel are fully aware that the family dynamic is dysfunctional and they choose to fight back. These children often face more wrath from abusers, but they also tend to have a better sense of self in the long run.

- Children who join play along, regardless of whether or not they recognize that something is not right. They are likely treated better because they follow directions and avoid rocking the boat, but they often struggle with their sense of identity whenever they leave home.
- Finally, in this case, freeze encompasses both the flight and freeze responses described above. These children may turn to escapism, compulsively distracting themselves through relationships, work, media, drugs, or other means, or dissociation, a mental detachment from reality.

ASSIGNING NEW ROLES TO THE HARGREEVES SIBLINGS

In this analysis, I will classify each of the living siblings into one of three roles: enforcers, rebels, and absentees. This is a new framework that looks to encompass family roles, trauma responses, and beliefs about the family system in a single classification system.

ENFORCERS: LUTHER AND ALLISON

The enforcers are Luther and Allison. Enforcers tend to join in with the abuser's toxic dynamic and justify harmful behavior. They are obedient, they police the other siblings, and they tend to react to conflict with fight and fawn responses. They believe it is better not to discuss the true magnitude of the abuse they experienced and its impact on all of them, but their exact response to these conversations can vary.

Luther is the most loyal to Sir Hargreeves and the familial status quo. With an anxious-avoidant attachment style, Luther becomes what clinicians sometimes call the "attacking" or "blaming" sibling[33]. He believes that his loyalty and self-sacrifice make him superior, so when his siblings complain, avoid problems, or try to leave altogether, he starts fights about their lack of commitment. Luther agreed to be stationed on the moon with no legitimate human contact for years, so he sees their complaints as comparatively irrelevant. All the siblings face his wrath at some point, but this especially creates conflict in his relationship with Diego, as they are essentially opposites.

Allison, meanwhile, is a "codependent agent"[34]. Throughout the season, she continually works to get everyone speaking to each other and pretending to be happy, without fully addressing the issues at hand. This often involves significantly changing her story and approach depending on context. In *Extra Ordinary*, she agrees with Diego's assertion that Viktor is a liability due to his lack of powers, though she is less rude about it. When Viktor is deeply hurt by that, she chastises Diego and insists she needs to go find Viktor and apologize[35]. Her desire to have the appearance of a functional family without doing the work nearly gets her killed — in *I Heard a Rumor*, her argument with Viktor starts with her dismissing his anger over her role in suppressing his powers. When she attempts to coerce Viktor into "mov[ing] on" (2019), he lashes out[36].

REBELS: DIEGO AND FIVE

The rebels are Diego and Five. They are fully aware that the dynamic amongst the siblings is toxic and they are loud about it, as they are completely disinterested in validation or approval from the family system. Opposite from the enforcers, they see buying into their father's narratives as naive and pathetic, and they are waiting for their other siblings to "wake up." This results in a stronger sense of self, but also a sense of constant conflict. Unsurprisingly, they usually turn to the fight response.

Diego constantly criticizes his siblings for their life choices, yet he is seemingly the most upset about Viktor airing everyone's dirty laundry in his memoir. Considering his disgust with the family system, some of the anger may come from being humiliated in public rather than just a violation of privacy. While he chooses to fight with his siblings, there are elements of flight in his relationship with Detective Patch due to his fearful-avoidant attachment style. He values the relationship but simultaneously dodges anything approaching vulnerability as it terrifies him.

Five is a scapegoat who disobeyed and paid the ultimate price. During his teenage years, Sir Hargreeves insisted that time travel was too dangerous, even if Five felt confident that he could do it. Eventually, he did it anyway, and after a few successful jumps, he got stuck in a post-apocalyptic future. When he returns to the main timeline, his perspective is undeniably changed by the life he lived as an assassin for the Commission, but many of the hallmarks of both his rebel role amongst the siblings and his anxious-avoidant attachment style remain. He is convinced that he knows best and that the others' mess — which is how he perceives their relationships, motivations, and practical concerns — is a distraction from his ability to get the job done.

ABSENTEES: KLAUS AND VIKTOR

The absentees are Klaus and Viktor. They have the tendency to display flight and freeze responses, or more specifically, distract, dissociate, or disappear. They run from reality so intensely that they are not able to plan and instead float through their lives on a day-to-day basis. Absentees are conflict-avoidant, so they rarely take sides and prefer to not be present at all. Additionally, absentees are at high risk for addiction to whatever coping strategies most consistently help them check out of their own lives.

Early in season one, Klaus leans heavily into the distract strategy, taking something of a mascot or clown role. He over-performs wildly shifting emotions in a blatant attempt to redirect attention whenever the tension in the room gets too high, to the exasperation of his siblings who are constantly interrupted by unhelpful commentary.

Additionally, while his substance use is directly tied to the supernatural element of avoiding his powers, this is common amongst absentees and those who primarily respond to stress with flight. Unable to control his ability to perceive ghosts, he finds himself overwhelmed with spirits demanding his attention while sober. Substance use dampens his powers and provides a break from the distressing highjacking of his time and attention without his consent. The unregulated recreational substance use also creates a chaotic lifestyle that prevents him from having the time and space to reflect on his problems.

Viktor, meanwhile, is a classic "lost child"[37]. This term, often used to describe children of substance-using parents, takes on additional meaning as Viktor is often not present during family encounters, even when Klaus is. He is socially isolated, desperate for someone to care, and sleepwalking through life when the season opens. Additionally, Viktor is most likely substance dependent as well. The reflex to take a pill every time something vaguely upsetting happens suggests that his medication is an as-needed, benzodiazepine-like prescription that depresses his emotions (e.g. Xanax, Valium, or Ativan) rather than a mood stabilizer that would be taken once a day[38]. If we assume this medication functions similarly to a benzodiazepine, it would aid in creating a sense of constant partial dissociation that prevents Viktor from having to acknowledge how isolated, rejected, and incompetent he feels.

Assigning each sibling a role provides additional context on the feelings and desires that motivate each sibling's behavior. Additionally, each sibling has reason to think that what they experienced was the worst. Those who complied had to give up everything, those who did not faced the most anger and direct abuse, and those who were on the sidelines were the most neglected and shunned. To further analyze how these roles interact, I will now reflect on the specific dynamics among three of the siblings: Luther, Diego, and Klaus.

WHEN ROLES COLLIDE

LUTHER AND DIEGO: ENFORCER AND REBEL

Luther believes in the Umbrella Academy and what their father intended them to be, so he perceives Diego's rebellion as both selfish and ungrateful. He thinks his willingness to sacrifice a normal life for the cause is noble compared to his siblings who are more interested in chasing pleasure — Diego through his vigilante work that includes all of the rewarding parts of saving people with none of the challenges, Allison through her new celebrity life, Klaus through drug use, and Viktor through his book that brought him validation at the expense of his siblings. In multiple conversations, he suggests that Diego threw away his chance at a meaningful life due to emotional fragility as he could not handle being "Number Two."

Meanwhile, Diego perceives that loyalty as pathetic willful ignorance. From his perspective, staying at the Academy, living off of Reginald's money, and saying yes to any and all requests was taking the easy way out. His disgust for Luther is lined with pity — Luther's complete cluelessness about how the world works got him stranded on the moon for four years while the other siblings were establishing normal lives based on their interests. Like many rebels, Diego has a relatively black-and- white perspective on the family conflict. Luther defending Sir Hargreeves puts him on the side of the abuser and Diego responds in kind.

The enforcer/rebel dynamic is usually high-conflict because these two perceive each other as direct threats. The only way it deescalates is if one or both parties back down, which comes midway through the season for Luther and Diego.

In *The Day That Wasn't*, Luther finds all his mail from the moon shoved into a crawlspace, packing tape still intact[39]. Pogo suggests that Sir Hargreeves gave him the moon mission to "give him purpose", but Luther takes this as proof that Diego's assertions were correct — their father sent him away because he was not good enough, and this kept him out of sight and out of mind. On this day, which was undone by Five's time travel, Allison finds him after this revelation and comforts him. However, in *The Day That Was*, this leads Luther to go on a bender that is interrupted the next morning with a new revelation: their father was not murdered[40]. While Luther does not particularly trust Klaus' assertion that he spoke with their father through his powers, Five seems to accept this relatively easily, and Pogo confirms it to be the truth. Once again, their father has lied and manipulated his sense of duty to control him.

At this point, Luther must accept that Diego was right at least about their father's character and his willingness to use the children as pawns. Luther admits this when he and Diego next see each other while simultaneously saying that he is done with the family entirely. Diego informs him that Allison is in mortal peril and the whole thing is tabled in favor of the current crisis.

The development of this relationship in season one demonstrates how one person being proven right and the other one admitting it does not solve the problem. Sure, the fighting has paused and perhaps even stopped, but this is not the start of rebuilding a meaningful relationship between Luther and Diego. This is in large part because the short conversation they have is about their dad, not about each other. Luther and Diego do not make progress on understanding each other or addressing their past interactions, which prevents meaningful growth or change.

LUTHER AND KLAUS: ENFORCER AND ABSENTEE

Klaus and Luther's tension focuses on resilience and self-awareness rather than courage. Luther echoes his father's sentiment about Klaus: his brother has wasted his life due to his unwillingness to tolerate discomfort long enough to develop and control his power. Combined with Klaus' tendency to diffuse conflict through interruption and distraction, Luther finds his very presence infuriating. From his perspective as an enforcer, Klaus has taken the easy way out because he stands for nothing.

Klaus, meanwhile, seems to cycle between being irritated with Luther and pitying him. Luther's constant condescension is grating, but at the same time, there is condescension in the reverse direction as well. As an escapee, Klaus does not take sides in arguments when it does not serve him, but deep down he believes that their father was a loveless manipulator and Luther is too delusional to see it.

This creates a dynamic in which the two irritate each other in a cyclical fashion until Luther goes off the deep end after learning about the pointlessness of his moon mission. His insistence on going on a bender to forget his pain starts a 24-hour role reversal largely enforced by Ben, the now-deceased Number Six. Seemingly able to get through to Klaus regardless of his intoxication or lack thereof, he becomes the angel on Klaus' shoulder pushing him to follow through and help Luther. Therefore, while Luther gets drunk and runs off looking for trouble, Klaus chases after him despite being in acute withdrawal himself.

While the show takes pains to emphasize how thoroughly the two have metaphorically switched places — all the way down to Luther offering Klaus drugs — it has impressively little impact. Perhaps Luther forgets most of his night at the rave, but when Klaus wakes him up the next morning, Luther is back to his usual level of suspicion and derision. Klaus retreats to his role of side character by choice, and once Diego gets Luther motivated to rescue Allison, everything is back to normal.

In this case, Klaus and Luther presumably understand each other a little bit better after this incident. Luther knows what it is like to desperately want to stop feeling whatever the cost and Klaus has experienced the frustration and exhaustion of being "the responsible one." Yet, this is not enough to change the way the two interact with each other, in large part because an intellectual understanding of why someone behaves the way they do is not enough to heal a relationship. Family-based trauma is inherently rooted in violations of identity and safety[41]. One scholar wrote that while he understands the factors that led to his parents being distant, unstable, and abusive now that he has studied psychology, the memories of his parents reacting to his childhood distress with cruelty are still painful today.

While Klaus and Luther now better understand each other's positions, there is no acknowledgment of how they have hurt each other in the past and how they continue to do so in the present. Both tend to ignore or belittle each other's distress and concerns and without acknowledgment of that, there will be no moving forward in healing that relationship.

DIEGO AND KLAUS: REBEL AND ABSENTEE

At the start of the season, Diego and Klaus' resentment of each other is framed primarily around their different approaches to life after the Academy. Diego is proud of making it out while simultaneously being the only one who is still saving people and fighting the good fight. He is frustrated with Klaus who seemingly will not take anything seriously and refuses to get out of the way of those who do. To Diego, everyone is an ally or a hindrance — no shades of gray — and Klaus is more of an obstacle than anything. Meanwhile, Klaus sees Diego and Luther as opposite sides of the same coin, and they are both exhausting. Diego is perhaps sneakier and more impulsive than Klaus is, yet Diego sees this as appropriate in his case as it is for some greater good. From Klaus' perspective, however, there is no righteousness in Diego's constant fighting against the system. These two mostly ignore each other's behavior unless someone (usually Klaus) needs something, but the dynamic shifts when they begin talking about their separate pasts almost accidentally.

In *Number Five*, Diego calls attention to Klaus being even more erratic than usual, to which Klaus reveals that he has recently lost someone he loved and is struggling to cope. This seems to catch Diego, who has recently lost his maybe-girlfriend Detective Patch, off guard. The disclosure leads to him dropping the issue, though he does point out Klaus' ability to reconnect with his dead loved one through his powers.

Following this talk, Klaus helps Diego out of a tough situation with the Commission's assassins, and this seemingly opens the opportunity for redeveloping a sense of trust in this relationship. Both brothers demonstrate a willingness to try out something they normally would not do: Diego listens without immediately offering an unwanted judgment and Klaus stays mentally present long enough to be helpful in a crisis. While these behavior changes will not heal the relationship on their own, they do fundamentally shift the dynamic. Deciding to check their impulses, which takes effort, creates a baseline of mutual respect. It is weak to start, but it is enough to make meaningful conversations feel worthwhile. Those conversations, such as the one they have in *The Day That Wasn't* while Diego ties Klaus up to force him to sober up, work toward a sense of insight and understanding that are fundamental to healing a dysfunctional family relationship[42]. While this day is, of course, erased, a shifted dynamic is still visible in *The Day That Was*, suggesting such conversations could happen again.

CONCLUDING THOUGHTS

The first season of the *Umbrella Academy* reflects many of the realities faced by adult siblings who experienced trauma in the home as children. The siblings' varied attachment styles and family roles overlap and clash, creating conflict and misunderstanding, but the show hints at how reconciliation is possible through the development of the relationship between Diego and Klaus. While none of the siblings are truly "doing the work" at the scale that would be discussed in a real-world therapeutic context, Diego and Klaus get the closest and therefore have the closest thing to a functional relationship at the end of the season. Allison talks the most about getting the family to truly function as a family again, but her codependent agent approach only creates more conflict. Luther, Five, and Viktor are not particularly interested in trying to work things out as it seems impossible, in large part because none of them are willing to embrace vulnerability and they cannot imagine the others doing it either.

It is important to note that shared family roles do not necessarily make things easier. Having had the most positive relationship as teenagers, Luther and Allison attempt to pick up where they left off, but Luther's resistance to vulnerability leaves a lot unsaid. In *The Day That Wasn't*, their joyful reconnection seems based on ignoring the current issues rather than dealing with them. Meanwhile, Diego and Five are both conflict-seeking while wanting to handle the situation in different ways, and Viktor and Klaus are running from their problems somewhat in opposite directions.

While family roles and attachment styles help explain why certain characters think and act the way they do, the greatest chance for reconciliation exists between the siblings who are most willing to put in the effort to treat someone else more fairly. The show provides a thoughtful depiction of these real- life dynamics among the sci-fi and supernatural elements that define *The Umbrella Academy* and this creates an opportunity for education about these topics via pop culture.

NOTES

1. Hoffner, C. A., & Cohen, E. L. (2012). Responses to Obsessive Compulsive Disorder on Monk Among Series Fans: Parasocial Relations, Presumed Media Influence, and Behavioral Outcomes. *Journal of Broadcasting & Electronic Media, 56*(4), 650–668. https://doi.org/10.1080/08838151.2012.732136
2. 2. Dictionary.com. (2021, October 20). Parasocial relationship | Meaning & Origin | Dictionary.com.

Dictionary.Com. https://www.dictionary.com/e/tech-science/parasocial- relationship/

3. Briere, J., & Scott, C. (2015). Complex Trauma in Adolescents and Adults. *Psychiatric Clinics of North America, 38*(3), 517. https://doi.org/10.1016/j.psc.2015.05.004

4. Brewin, C. R. (2020). Complex post-traumatic stress disorder: A new diagnosis in ICD-11. *BJPsych Advances, 26*(3), 145–146. https://doi.org/10.1192/bja.2019.48

5. Briere, J., & Scott, C. (2015). Complex Trauma in Adolescents and Adults. *Psychiatric Clinics of North America, 38*(3), 517. https://doi.org/10.1016/j.psc.2015.05.004

6. American Psychiatric Association, & American Psychiatric Association (Eds.). (2013). *Diagnostic and statistical manual of mental disorders: DSM-5* (5th ed). American Psychiatric Association.

7. Briere, J., & Scott, C. (2015). Complex Trauma in Adolescents and Adults. *Psychiatric Clinics of North America, 38*(3), 517. https://doi.org/10.1016/j.psc.2015.05.004

8. Cunic, A. (2023, May 3). *Dysregulation: What It Means and How to Cope.* Verywell Mind. https://www.verywellmind.com/what-is- dysregulation-5073868

9. World Health Organization. (2023a, January). *6B40 Post traumatic stress disorder.* ICD-11 for Mortality and Morbidity Statistics. https://icd.who.int/browse11/l-m/en#/http://id.who.int/icd/ entity/2070699808

10. Brewin, C. R. (2020). Complex post-traumatic stress disorder: A new diagnosis in ICD-11. *BJPsych Advances, 26*(3), 145–146. https://doi.org/10.1192/bja.2019.48

11. ibid

12. ibid

13. World Health Organization. (2023b, January). *6B41 Complex post traumatic stress disorder.* ICD-11 for Mortality and Morbidity Statistics. https://icd.who.int/browse11/l-m/en#/http://id.who.int/ icd/entity/585833559

14. ibid

15. Brewin, C. R. (2020). Complex post-traumatic stress disorder: A new diagnosis in ICD-11. *BJPsych Advances, 26*(3), 145–146. https://doi.org/10.1192/bja.2019.48

16. van der Kolk, B. A., & Pynoos, R. S. (2009). *Proposal to Include a Developmental Trauma Disorder Diagnosis for Children and Adolescents in DSM-V.*

17. Mikulincer, M., & Shaver, P. R. (2019). An attachment perspective on family relations. In *APA handbook of contemporary family psychology: Foundations, methods, and contemporary issues across the lifespan, Vol. 1* (pp. 109–125). American Psychological Association. https://doi.org/10.1037/0000099-007

18. Reis, S., & Grenyer, B. F. S. (2004). Fearful attachment, working alliance and treatment response for individuals with major depression. *Clinical Psychology & Psychotherapy, 11*(6), 414–424. https://doi.org/10.1002/cpp.428

19. Neese, J., Neese, J., Blackman, S., King, J., Goldberg, K., & Richardson, M. (Executive Producers). (2019). Season 1. In *The Umbrella Academy.* Netflix.

20. Shemmings, D., & Shemmings, Y. (2011). *Understanding Disorganized Attachment: Theory and Practice for Working with Children and Adults.* Jessica Kingsley Publishers

21. Reis, S., & Grenyer, B. F. S. (2004). Fearful attachment, working alliance and treatment response for individuals with major depression. *Clinical Psychology & Psychotherapy, 11*(6), 414–424. https://doi.org/10.1002/cpp.428

22. ibid

23. Lisitsa, E. (2013, May 20). *The Four Horsemen: Stonewalling*. The Gottman Institute. https://www.gottman.com/blog/the-four- horsemen-stonewalling/
24. Shemmings, D., & Shemmings, Y. (2011). *Understanding Disorganized Attachment: Theory and Practice for Working with Children and Adults.* Jessica Kingsley Publishers
25. Kramer, L., Conger, K. J., Rogers, C. R., & Ravindran, N. (2019). Siblings. In B. H. Fiese, M. Celano, K. Deater-Deckard, E. N. Jouriles, & M. A. Whisman (Eds.), *APA handbook of contemporary family psychology: Foundations, methods, and contemporary issues across the lifespan (Vol. 1).* (Vol. 1, pp. 521–538). American Psychological Association. https://doi.org/10.1037/0000099-029
26. Whiteman, S. D., Becerra, J. M., & Killoren, S. E. (2009). Mechanisms of sibling socialization in normative family development. *New Directions for Child and Adolescent Development, 2009*(126), 30–31. https://doi.org/10.1002/cd.255
27. ibid
28. Neese, J., Neese, J., Blackman, S., King, J., Goldberg, K., & Richardson, M. (Executive Producers). (2019). Season 1. In *The Umbrella Academy*. Netflix.
29. Kramer, L., Conger, K. J., Rogers, C. R., & Ravindran, N. (2019). Siblings. In B. H. Fiese, M. Celano, K. Deater-Deckard, E. N. Jouriles, & M. A. Whisman (Eds.), *APA handbook of contemporary family psychology: Foundations, methods, and contemporary issues across the lifespan (Vol. 1).* (Vol. 1, pp. 521–538). American Psychological Association. https://doi.org/10.1037/0000099-029
30. ibid
31. Walker, P. (2013). *The 4Fs: A Trauma Typology in Complex PTSD*. Pete Walker, M.A. Psychotherapy. http://www.pete-walker.com/ fourFs_TraumaTypology-ComplexPTSD.htm

32. Wright, A. (2019, July 7). Siblings can cope with trauma differently. Here's why. *Annie Wright, LMFT*. https://www.anniewright.com/ siblings-cope-with-trauma-differently/

33. Teahan, P. (Director). (2022, January 26). *8 Types of Sibling Issues From Childhood Trauma*. https://www. youtube.com/watch?v=Vo59czUVSuc

34. ibid

35. Neese, J., Neese, J., Blackman, S., King, J., Goldberg, K., & Richardson, M. (Executive Producers). (2019). Season 1. In *The Umbrella Academy*. Netflix.

36. ibid

37. Alvernia University. (2019). *Coping With Addiction: 6 Dysfunctional Family Roles*. Alvernia Online. https://online. alvernia.edu/ infographics/coping-with-addiction-6-dysfunctional-family-roles/

38. Pope, C. (2023). *List of Common Benzodiazepines Uses & Side Effects*. Drugs.Com. https://www.drugs.com/drug-class/ benzodiazepines.html

39. Neese, J., Neese, J., Blackman, S., King, J., Goldberg, K., & Richardson, M. (Executive Producers). (2019). Season 1. In *The Umbrella Academy*. Netflix.

40. ibid

41. Hargrave, T. D., & Zasowski, N. E. (2016). *Families and Forgiveness: Healing Wounds in the Intergenerational Family* (Second). Taylor & Francis.

42. ibid

WHY DO WE NOT LOVE ALL THE HARGREEVES' SIBLINGS THE SAME?

MICHELLE MÖRI AND ANDREAS FAHR

All around the world, millions of viewers engaged with the seven Hargreeves' siblings, protagonists of the popular TV show The Umbrella Academy. Luther, Diego, Allison, Klaus, Five, Ben, and Viktor were born the same night and adopted by Reginald Hargreeves, an eccentric billionaire. Each of the siblings is endowed with a specific superpower. Trained by Reginald, they use these powers in various scenarios to protect the world from evil. After Reginald's mysterious death, the rather dysfunctional family of superheroes comes together to protect the world, among other objectives, from an imminent apocalypse with their supernatural powers. Throughout the three seasons, the siblings are confronted with individual traumas from their past, dysfunctional family dynamics, and attacks from The Sparrow Academy. The Sparrow Academy also consists of seven "children" born on the same day and are also adopted by Reginald Hargreeves. Their existence arose following a change in the timeline caused by The Umbrella Academy. The Sparrow Academy is almost identical to The Umbrella Academy but built with what Hargreeves believes to be a better set of children. Viewers of The Umbrella Academy invest hours of their time watching the adventures of the seven Hargreeves siblings because they enjoy their stories and feel well entertained.

But what do we exactly enjoy about watching these superheroes who struggle with their lives while trying to save the world from an emerging apocalypse? Why do we like them despite their often immoral behavior? Why don`t we like all siblings in the same way? The following chapter will provide answers to these questions. First, we explain why viewers like or dislike media characters and why they even consider some of these fictional superheroes, such as the Hargreeves, as their friends. Then, we discuss what makes the Hargreeves' siblings attractive as parasocial friends and why viewers relate differently to the seven siblings. Further, we present the findings of a study among viewers of The Umbrella Academy to explore which Hargreeves are the most liked and the most popular as parasocial friends.

WHY DO WE CONSIDER FICTIONAL AND SUPERNATURAL MEDIA CHARACTERS AS OUR FRIENDS?

Media characters are important to us. They drive the stories, draw us into the narrative, and take us on their journey. Media characters connect the fictional world and viewers' emotions, experiences, and values. We, as viewers, are wired to connect with and relate to those characters, like we tend to connect with people around us in everyday life. Through meaningful connections with media characters, viewers can dive into fictional worlds, escape their daily lives, and experience events through a character's perspective that they would never encounter in their real lives. Supplementing our daily experiences with adventurous media characters or trustworthy friends increases our entertainment experience[1]. Thus, when viewers of The Umbrella Academy feel like friends with the Hargreeves siblings and the siblings succeed in their battles, they feel entertained. At the same time, they think entertained when their antagonists from The Sparrow Academy fail in their endeavors[2]. If their favorite sibling fails, they are disappointed – but full of hope that they will succeed next time. So, come on, let`s watch another episode.

How do these relationships between fictional media characters such as the Hargreeves and ordinary viewers develop? When watching a TV show such as The Umbrella Academy, viewers observe the actions of the portrayed protagonists; they quickly form an opinion about them and build positive or negative affective dispositions toward them. For example, after the first episode in the first season, most viewers have already thought about which of the Hargreeves they like or dislike. Those positive feelings stem from a combination of relatability, depth, growth, likability, moral integrity, resonance, or memorable qualities. Such spontaneous liking can develop into stronger feelings depending on the characters' development. For example, if you became a fan of Klaus starting with Season 1, Episode 1, and you watched all the following episodes and liked what he did or said, your positive feelings toward Klaus presumably increased. Parasocial relationships[3] are what researchers describe as feelings of friendship with a character you only know from the media. The prefix "para-" means "beside" or "alongside." It stands for the one-sidedness or asymmetry in this relationship. Thus, you can also have a fictional media character like Klaus as your friend, your parasocial friend1.

WHAT DIFFERENTIATES FRIENDSHIPS FROM PARASOCIAL RELATIONSHIPS?

Parasocial relationships might seem a little odd at first sight: Klaus is a fictional media character who lives in a fictional world, changes timelines with ease, dies, uses supernatural powers, and engages in epic fight battles. Compared to real-life social friendships, he is undoubtedly different from friends from school or work[4]. For example, he can never directly react to us; we will never exchange text messages with him; he will never give us concrete advice on how to handle a difficult situation with our boss or what to do after a romantic breakup. In real- world relationships, there is typically a mutual exchange of thoughts, feelings, and actions between individuals. Thus, "real" relationships allow for dialogue, negotiation, and conflict resolution. Real relationships involve physical proximity and interaction, including face-to-face communication and touch. Real relationships often involve shared experiences and intimate knowledge of each other's lives. Real-world relationships can provide emotional support, companionship, and validation during times of need. Personal growth, life events, and external circumstances influence them. At the same time, they are governed by social norms, expectations, and ethical considerations.

In contrast, there is no actual reciprocity in parasocial relationships since the relationship is one-sided. The audience member invests emotions and attention into the character, but the character does not really reciprocate. The mediated experiences through screens or other forms of media lack physical presence and interaction. Through that, relationships with media characters are usually considered more superficial, as they are limited to the audience's interpretation of the character's actions, dialogue, and behaviors without the opportunity for direct communication or interaction. Moreover, parasocial relationships do not offer the same level of social support, as characters are fictional constructs and not capable of providing real-world assistance or empathy[3,4]. Because the writers and creators predetermine the character's traits, behaviors, and storylines, parasocial relationships cannot be developed by the viewer.

Still, parasocial relationships are also characterized similarly to social relationships in some points; for example, these relationships can vary in intensity, change over time, and result in breakups[4]. Referring to our parasocial relationship with Klaus, this means that we can have a stronger relationship with him from time to time. We might distance ourselves from him when he acts out or does something immoral that we condemn. However, when he returns to acting as usual, we might intensify our relationship again. In contrast, if something Klaus says or does really bothers us, we might also decide to break up our friendship with him, as we might do when the same happens with a real social friend.

THE HARGREEVES' SIBLINGS AS OUR IDEAL PARASOCIAL FRIENDS?

When you think about it, media characters could be ideal friends. Classic movie heroes like *Robin Hood or Superman* are always good and protect the world from evil. Or we think about talented people with powers we do not have, such as *Harry Potter*, a powerful wizard, or *Wonder Woman*, a master combatant and warrior princess. Maybe we do not only want to have one parasocial friend but rather join an entire group, such as being friends with *Phoebe, Chandler, Joey, Rachel*, and *Ross* from *Friends*. More generally, media characters seem ideal parasocial friends because they have suitable characteristics. For example, they are very reliable. If the media characters act predictably, their behavior becomes familiar and forms a reliable source for the viewers. Predictability can increase viewers' sense of belonging, decrease their loneliness, and offer them connections to others in the safe space of a mediated context. Having parasocial friendships is much less time-consuming than real social friendships, with people who expect you to invest time and commitment in your common relationships. With only a few touches on a digital device, your favorite episode with your parasocial friend is on, and you can foster your relationship wherever you are or whenever you want.

However, being predictable and heroic actions are not always crucial. A special feature of The Umbrella Academy is that the show does not match the classical "hero fights and defeats the villain in the end"- blueprint. Sure, the siblings pursue the noble goal of trying to save the world. However, to achieve their goal, they also engage in immoral behavior. Here, the classic trope of what Kant called "rationality of purpose" is skillfully played with. The viewer is repeatedly put in a quandary: Is it okay to act this way? Would I act the same way? Should I rethink my attitude towards Luther? Or can I still like him?

Throughout the show, the Hargreeves engage in a wide range of immoral behavior, such as emotional or substance abuse, selfishness, aggression, or manipulation. For example, Viktor becomes increasingly unstable and dangerous in Season 2, which reaches its peak when he tortures a person by using his powers to induce excruciating pain to get information from him. The other person is just an innocent bystander at the wrong place at the wrong time and suffers from Viktor's use of his supernatural power. Another example of Hargreeves engaging in immoral behavior is Allison. The most significant example of Allison's immoral behavior is the use of her powers to manipulate her daughter's emotions and behavior. She repeatedly tells her daughter, Claire, "I heard a rumor that you think I'm the best mom ever," effectively controlling Claire's thoughts. This manipulation becomes a source of tension between Allison and her husband as he becomes aware of her misuse of power.

However, these immoral behaviors do not necessarily lead viewers to avoid the Hargreeves as parasocial friends. Studies have shown that viewers form parasocial relationships with media characters such as antagonists, villains, or morally ambiguous media characters [56]. In fact, viewers likely develop parasocial relationships with the Hargreeves siblings despite – or even because – their immoral behaviors, their flaws, and shortcomings. Like most of us, the siblings are morally ambiguous characters, which makes them "human" and relatable. It is precisely these uncertainties that generate attention and suspense.

WHY DO WE NOT LIKE ALL THE HARGREEVES THE SAME?

Why do we like some of the siblings so much while we just roll our eyes at the others and get annoyed each time they appear in an episode? With seven protagonists in The Umbrella Academy, viewers likely do not like all the Hargreeves the same, and they do not want to befriend all of them. The Hargreeves are all superheroes with supernatural powers and share the same background story of being born on the same day and adopted by an emotionless father. At the same time, they are also very different from each other. For example, Luther, as the oldest sibling, is disciplined and responsible, follows the rules, and often takes on leadership roles. In contrast, Klaus is a free spirit, disobeys authorities, and generally acts rebellious. Allison is compassionate and empathetic and usually supports her siblings and other loved ones emotionally.

We become attracted to different characters because of our individual history, personality traits, or personal needs. We might see elements of ourselves, or our own experiences, reflected in media characters, making them relatable and creating a sense of connection. Watching this character evolve and grow throughout a story can be rewarding and satisfying, leading us to root for this one Hargreeves and feel invested in their journey. In particular, characters such as the Hargreeves with layered personalities, motivations, and backstories are compelling to viewers. They evoke strong emotions through their personal struggles, triumphs, or relationships, fostering a deep emotional attachment. Characters who embody courage, kindness, integrity, or justice can resonate with our individual values and ideals, leading us to admire them. As the Hargreeves are very different, they attract different viewers. Simply put, there is "somebody for everyone". This was crucial for the show's success in reaching a broad audience worldwide.

WHICH HARGREEVES ARE LIKED AND POPULAR AS PARASOCIAL FRIENDS AMONG VIEWERS?

After looking for theoretically derived reasons why the Hargreeves are liked and popular as parasocial friends, we wanted to know more about viewers' actual (dis-)liking of the Hargreeves siblings, as well as their parasocial relationships with them. To explore this – and to have more than just personal and anecdotal evidence for the liking of the Hargreeves siblings – we asked 550 viewers of the first three seasons about their feelings toward the Hargreeves. Thereby, we were interested in two things. First, we wanted to know how much they liked or disliked each of the seven siblings. Second, we asked them if they would describe the siblings as their friends in the sense of parasocial relationships that we described previously[7].

VIEWERS GENERALLY LIKE ALL HARGREEVES

Based on the data of this survey, viewers did not indicate extremely low liking for any of the seven Hargreeves siblings. This shows that these imperfect heroes – who cross several moral boundaries and engage in heavy battles while also caring for each other and trying to save the world – are liked despite their shortcomings and immoral behaviors.

The differences in the general liking of the Hargreeves overall the viewers are relatively small between the siblings. This is interesting, as viewers seem to have strong opinions about the Hargreeves. Every viewer appears to have a clear favorite, and one of the siblings is the especially bothersome one. However, it seems that, overall, these preferences are very individual, so none of the Hargreeves siblings can be clearly labeled as generally disliked by all viewers of The Umbrella Academy. When focusing on the feelings of being friends with them, again, no significant differences between the seven Hargreeves emerge. Some viewers perceive all of them as good parasocial friends, others perceive none of them as essential, and others have a clear favorite.

We now take a closer look at each of the seven siblings. In the following paragraphs, we present the viewers' evaluations of each of the seven siblings and show some surprising differences between viewers' liking of them and their wish to befriend them.

WHY DO WE LOVE KLAUS SO MUCH?

Among the viewers we asked, Klaus was the most liked among the seven siblings. This might not be surprising to many of you, or was it? Of the seven Hargreeves, viewers also had the second most intense parasocial relationship with Klaus. Thus, Klaus can really be considered one of the favorite siblings. What makes viewers like him and want to be friends, and what differentiates him from the other siblings?

Klaus often shows humor with witty remarks and sarcasm. He displays personal growth, and he seems vulnerable through the portrayal of his troubles with addiction and trauma. While Klaus may not always seem fair in his actions, he does care about his family and can show compassion and loyalty in his own unique way. Despite his flaws, he tries to contribute positively to the group dynamics, even if it's not always in the most conventional manner. This visibility of his shortcomings and personal development might make viewers relate to and like him. Klaus is reliable, viewers know what to expect from him, and he seems generally good even though he sometimes struggles. The notion of "relatable superheroes," often used for the Hargreeves, perfectly fits him.

WE LIKE FIVE BUT DON'T WANT TO BE FRIENDS WITH HIM

Besides Klaus, Five is the next most liked of the Hargreeves among our interviewed viewers. This is not surprising, as Five is often considered a fan favorite in public discussions and social media platforms,[8],[9]. So, what is it that makes viewers like him so much? Five is intelligent and always strives to accomplish his goals, such as preventing the apocalypse. He is caring, especially toward his family, and shows a lot of compassion. He is hard- working and engaged in saving his family and avoiding the apocalypse, especially in Season 2. For example, when he renegotiates his contract with the Temps Commission, he tries to save all family members. However, Five is haunted by traumatic events and struggles emotionally. He shows antisocial behavior and is a killing machine. He eliminates innocent people if he thinks that their deaths could stop the apocalypse, and he does not show any signs of compassion towards them. When it suits his interests, Five disregards rules and authorities. For example, he endangers the family's mission with his solo mission. In Season 3, finally, he seeks peace and accepts his fate despite the emerging apocalypse.

Interestingly, when looking at viewers' feelings of friendship, Five is not among the most preferred siblings, even though he was the most liked. It seems that viewers like dazzling and manifold characters such as Five but do not want someone like him to be a friend. This is revealing because it shows that a character can be liked, but this does not have to result in a friend- like relationship. In the case of Five, the many solo missions and killing of innocent bystanders could have led to viewers not wanting him as a parasocial friend while they still agreed on liking him.

LUTHER IS LIKED AND POPULAR AS A PARASOCIAL FRIEND

Well, that Klaus and Five are strongly liked is probably not surprising. Besides these two, our interviewed viewers also liked Luther quite well and could imagine being friends with him. For Luther, the viewers' liking and wish to be parasocial friends with him are congruent. He is among the most liked and among the most preferred as fictional friends. It seems that viewers like Luther and, in turn, are motivated to have him as their friend. Understandably, viewers think they can especially trust him when they perceive him as likable, encouraging them to befriend him. Hence, why are viewers so optimistic about him?

Generally, this liking and friendship with Luther show that a complex character with various strengths and flaws can be liked and perceived as positive. As the oldest of the siblings, Luther is intensely loyal to his siblings and acts very protective of his family. Viewers perceive him as very loyal to friends and family. He is powerful, faithful, and engaged. Luther sacrifices his fighter career to help his siblings prevent the apocalypse and puts the general needs over his own priorities. Like his siblings, Luther is shown as struggling. For example, when he comes back after his four-year mission on the moon and finds out that Reginald never read any of the reports that he used to send to him, he thinks that he was sent away because he was not good enough as Number One. This drastically decreased his self-confidence. However, this prevalence of his struggles and self-criticism might increase viewers' liking of him, making him seem relatable despite his supernatural powers. His loving, protective, and engaged behavior for the family might lead viewers to think of him as an ideal parasocial friend on which they can count in times of need.

WE WANT VIKTOR AS A FRIEND BUT DO NOT ESPECIALLY LIKE HIM

Viktor is not particularly liked or disliked by the viewers. However, together with Klaus and Luther, viewers have the strongest desire to be friends with Viktor. Interestingly, here we have the opposite situation: While Viktor might not trigger strong affective dispositions toward himself, viewers would want to befriend him. What could make Viktor so attractive as a parasocial friend?

Viktor is kind, bright, and cares a lot about his loved ones, especially about Sissy and her son Harlan. Viktor tries to act fairly and advocates justice for people who have been wronged. Since he was not initially accepted, he does not have solid loyalty to the family. In Season 1, when he does not know his powers, he feels like an outcast and is very vulnerable and naïve. He became mighty when he recognized his power, which changed his self- esteem. But he shows himself to be harmful when he uses his supernatural power. In Season 2, he starts healing all his trauma. However, he becomes increasingly unstable and dangerous. He makes an immoral decision when he tortures an innocent person by using his powers to induce excruciating pain to get information from him. Thus, his unstable personality traits, traumatic solid past, and struggle to overcome it might decrease viewers' liking of him. However, viewers might consider him an excellent parasocial friend because of his caring, engagement with loved ones, and effort to become a better person.

DIEGO, ALLISON, AND BEN DID NOT EVOKE STRONG RESPONSES

The siblings Diego, Allison, and Ben are neither liked nor viewers' favorites as friends. This can be due to several reasons. All three of them are often presented as having struggles connecting with others. Emotional distance could be one reason viewers want to avoid connecting with them as friends. Diego's impulsiveness or anger, leading him to lash out quite often, could also decrease viewers' connection with him. Ben is dead before the start of the series; however, still sometimes present through visions, as a statue counterpart, or with Klaus. Ben is very introverted, and he does not seem to like being in the company of many other people. Allison often acts guarded and reserved in emotions; she strongly focuses on her needs with a sense of self-centeredness and has a problem with forgiveness. These characteristics could decrease viewers' deeper connections with them.

However, as with the other siblings, Diego, Allison, and Ben also show personal development and moral decisions. For example, in Season 2, Episode 3, Allison makes an ethical decision when she stops a racist owner of a diner from assaulting a black customer. Despite being tempted to use her power of whispering to manipulate the situation, she uses her words to reason with the diner owner and prevent him from causing harm. In Season 2, Diego is obsessed with his desire to change history by saving President Kennedy, and he is even prepared to sacrifice his own life for this endeavor. Ben is also described as the moral compass for Klaus, who often refuses to listen. Still, their personal growth and moral actions did not lead viewers to form strong likings or feelings of friendships towards them.

What could be the reasons for that? In general, characters who undergo significant development, growth, and internal struggles tend to resonate more deeply with viewers. Five, Klaus, and Luther have complex story arcs that explore their personal demons, relationships, and inner conflicts, which allow viewers to connect with them on a deeper level. They each have distinct personality traits and struggles that viewers may find relatable, such as feelings of isolation, identity crises, or family dynamics. The three often play central roles in the plot, with significant screen time dedicated to their storylines and character development. Finally, they have compelling dynamics with other members of *The Umbrella Academy* and external characters, which enhance their likability and complexity. In contrast, Diego, Allison, and Ben receive less focus or development in certain seasons, leading to a weaker emotional connection. They may not always have as many relatable characteristics or experiences, making it harder for viewers to empathize with them. The three of them play less prominent roles and have fewer opportunities to shine, making it harder for viewers to form strong bonds with them. Finally, Diego, Allison, and Ben do not have as many dynamic relationships or interactions that capture viewers' attention. Thus, these could all be reasons for the lower liking and relationships with them.

CONCLUSION: THE HARGREEVES SIBLINGS AND MORALITY

Millions of viewers watched the show The Umbrella Academy. The seven Hargreeves siblings offer a wide diversity of characters with which viewers can connect and interact. In the mediated world, generally, viewers strive to connect with media characters by connecting with them, empathizing with their flaws, or admiring their growth1. This seeking of a connection with media characters does not necessarily mean that viewers also want to be friends with them. While viewers may enjoy spending time with a media character, they may feel that they need more in common to sustain a meaningful friendship3. In this chapter, viewers' liking and their feelings of friend-like relationships with the seven Hargreeves siblings were discussed. Viewers formed positive parasocial relationships, especially with Luther and Klaus. While Five was among the most liked of the siblings, this general liking did not result in stronger parasocial relationships. In contrast, Viktor was popular as a parasocial friend but not especially liked by viewers. Thus, the mere liking of fictional media characters does not have to result in viewers' desire to be friends with them, and the Hargreeves siblings triggered different feelings of liking and friendship in viewers worldwide.

NOTES

1. Klimmt C., Hartmann T., & Schramm H. (2006) *Parasocial Interactions and Relationships*. In: Bryant J, Vorderer P, eds. Psychology of Entertainment. Lawrence Erlbaum Associates Publishers, 291-313.
2. Zillmann D., Cantor J.R. (1977) Affective responses to the emotions of a protagonist. *Journal of Experimental Social Psychology, 13*(2),155-165. doi:10.1016/S0022-1031(77)80008-5
3. Tukachinsky R. (2011) Para-romantic love and para-friendships: Development and assessment of a multiple-parasocial relationships scale. *American Journal of Media Psychology*, 3(1/2), 73-94.
4. Klimmt, C., Hartmann, T., & Schramm, H. (2006). Parasocial interactions and relationships. In J. Bryant & P. Vorderer (Eds.), *Psychology of entertainment* (pp. 291–313). Lawrence Erlbaum Associates Publishers.

5. Brodie Z.P., Ingram J. (2021) The dark triad of personality and hero/ villain status as predictors of parasocial relationships with comic book characters. *Psycholy of Popular Media*, 10(2), 230-242. doi:10.1037/ppm0000323

6. Tian Q., & Hoffner C. (2010) Parasocial interaction with liked, neutral, and disliked characters on a popular TV series. *Mass Communication and Society,13*(3), 250-269.

7. More about our empirical study can be found here: https://osf.io/ u5h9p/

8. Nason M. Umbrella Academy: 8 Most Likable Characters (& 7 Fans Can't Stand). ScreenRant. Published September 16, 2020. Accessed April 13, 2023. https://screenrant.com/ netflix-umbrella-academy- likable-characters/

9. Nguyen J. "The Umbrella Academy": 10 Best Episodes That Made Number Five A Fan-Favorite. Collider. Published October 27, 2022. Accessed April 13, 2023. https://collider.com/the-umbrella- academy-10-best-episodes-that-made-number-five-a-fan-favorite/

AN UNLIKELY PAIR: FIVE AND DELORES

EMORY S. DANIEL, PHD

Parasocial relationships (PSR) is a term used to refer to the one-sided relationships we form with media figures of all kinds – both real (e.g., movie stars and rock stars[1]) or fictional[2] (e.g., the Hargreeves family). The idea is that through continued exposure to "media figures" we start to form real emotional relationships with them. We may start to admire them, celebrate their success, and grieve alongside their losses. While the social relationship is not a traditional one, the emotions associated with it very much are. Parasocial relationships help explain why we feel sad that Luther was sent to the moon, share Klaus' fear when he is locked in the tomb, and lament over the lost years Five spent wandering the post-apocalyptic wasteland with Delores.

That last example is of particular interest. While researchers of fandom and parasocial relationships have a good understanding of the parasocial relationships between viewer and subject of viewers' adoration, there has been less discussion around the implications of a fictional character demonstrating a parasocial relationship in their story. In most examples of cinema and television, the implications are that someone loves the "idea" of someone (e.g. a romantic crush) has a negative or dangerous obsession with someone (e.g. fandom) or has a relationship with an AI. However, we cannot talk about parasocial relationships in television without talking about the relationship between Five and Delores.

PARASOCIAL RELATIONSHIPS

If you have heard the term Parasocial Relationships, it may be linked with negative perceptions of fandom being too close with public figures. However, it is important to remember that everyone amongst us exhibits some form of parasocial relationships (PSR). Afterall, who doesn't get attached to fictional characters, identify with their mannerisms or feels pain when a character passes away? If you imagine your favorite member of the Hargreeves family, I imagine that you could do so very quickly. We engage in this behavior because we have the same goals with PSR as we do in actual relationships. We often flock to people who have similar characteristics that we have. For example, one of my favorite characters is Diego because I identify with his personality. I find myself wanting to be protective of my friends but carry around insecurities about by abilities. These attributes that Diego and I share make for a bond that I have with the character.

The relationships that we form with mediated fictional characters can often play an important role in our lives[3]. We spend a great deal of time watching shows and movies, and, consequently, connecting to the lives personalities of the characters on screen[4]. These parasocial relationships between us and the characters we watch often translate into emotional connections and reactions towards the characters[5]. Our frustration with Klaus's relationship with his cult, the sympathy we share when Diego tries to humanize Grace, or the anger we share with Sir Reginald Hargreeves treatment of his children, these are all examples of our PSR with the characters of *The Umbrella Academy*.

What is particularly interesting about PSR is we feel like we are having an interaction with these characters even though they do not respond to us from the other side of the screen. Some of the most original research of PSR and interactions stems from the relationships that people would develop towards television news anchors, which in part was due to the illusion of connection that the anchor made while he/she was staring at the camera[6]. This also creates an illusion of presence, where a news anchor actually feels present in the room[7]. While a similar effect can be made when actors break the fourth wall, even without this assumed "direct" communication, we begin to form social and emotional bonds with the characters we are watching on the screen. Parasocial relationships are unique in this way, because they form and exist regardless of any overt interaction between the us, the viewer, and them, the character[8].

The strength of these relationships do seem to be, at least partially, related to just sheer exposure. The more viewers watch actual people and fictional characters it increases the liking and credibility of that persona. As such, parasocial relationships tend to develop over a period of time[9] and come with a sense of longevity. The more we encounter a character, the greater chance we may form a parasocial relationship with them. Over time, I felt more and more compassion with Five and the horrible atrocities that he faced in a post-apocalyptic wasteland all by himself. Some behaviors that seemed dismissive and cynical before were excused given his traumatic circumstances. I may not have felt that way without subsequent views of the show. However, it is important to understand we do not form parasocial relationships with *all* of the characters we see on a screen. For example, In I never felt attached to Luther as a character. As big as his presence is, he never stood out to me as the other Hargreeves children did. All of us likely have a story like that where we feel indifferent about a character and press on. Or the behavior of a character might become so frustrating that viewers might want to stop watching all together In these cases, we could say an interaction is present but not a relationship[10] (I'm looking at you Reginald Hargreeves). What distinguishes a relationship from an interaction is that parasocial relationships extend beyond the viewing period[11]. Our parasocial relationships with the Hargreeves children Iare what keeps us thinking about them long after the show is over.

Unfortunately, all television series and, therefore, the relationships with characters, will ultimately come to an end. Similar to social relationships, the breakup with a fictional character is a negative experience[12,13,14,15]. Research had found that if a viewer had a strong friendship tie towards a character, and the character left, died, or the show ended, more negative emotion was experienced[16]. However, much like with social relationships, the strength of the relationship determined how much distress the viewer had undergone. For example, while viewers might feel some contempt that Pogo was withholding information about Reginald's death, there was a sense of loss with Pogo when he was killed by the White Violin. Given Pogo's fatherly demeanor to the children, and the hardships that he went through, viewers might feel loss and sadness for him. People experience this while watching a show. Notably, not all breakups are equal and characters who we have positive emotions towards will elicit stronger emotions[17].

GOING META: THE STORY OF FIVE AND DELORES

As mentioned at the start of this chapter, media researchers understand and know a lot about how parasocial relationships operate. While we often talk about them as *our* relationships with *others*, it is very rare for us to witness a parasocial relationship being portrayed back at us. The story of Five and Delores is a notable exception.

Five is one of the seven Hargreeves children that were adopted by Sir Reginald Hargreeves. Like his siblings, he was gifted extraordinary powers. Five's superpower allows him to jump through space and time. While he seemingly teleports from place to place in the present world he exists in, he is also curious about time travel into the past and future. Five eventually leaves home and explores time travel under his own accord and travels into the future which ultimately that leaves him in the middle of a post-apocalyptic timeline where all of his siblings have died. What's worse, is he is unable to travel back in time. Five is alone in the world.

At this time, Five goes to procure a newspaper with the date of Apocalypse on it. Upon arrival, he spots a mannequin whose lower body was removed. Having no one else to talk to, Five brings the mannequin, now named Delores, to accompany him for 40 years on their journey through a now desolate earth.

While Five and Delores do not drive a significant plot point in the show, it is an important dynamic of Five's character growth and development. Five is not only desperate for any sort of interaction, he comes to the realization that he may never have another entity to talk to than Delores. As parasocial relationships are inherently one-way emotional investments (obviously, Delores cannot reciprocate Five's affection towards him), Five must create all of the attributes and emotions concerning the PSR that he has for her. Similarly to how we, as viewers, tend to attribute personality traits from characters to the actor playing them (what do you mean Aidan Gallagher does not speak in the same cadence as Five?)[18,19], Five must "fill in the blanks" about Delores.

While not apparent in the show, The Umbrella Academy graphic novel paints a very striking picture for maybe why Five develops attachment to, not only Delores, but why he may be attached to a mannequin. First off, mannequins are considered to be humanoid, and many look very similar to an actual person. Another similarity is that in the graphic novel, the character Mom also resembles a staging mannequin. And while Five has shown stark contempt toward Grace aka "Mom"—partly for not being a real person—it appears that Five projects love on an actual object, who is similar to one of the only familiar members that ever showed him affection. While this anecdote is not canon, it does support that Five would project affection and personality based on something from his past. In turn, Five treats objects more like people than he does actual people.

As viewers, we learn that during his years with Delores, he creates her personality, interaction, and style (e.g., Five states that Delores loves sequins). Since it is clear that Delores is an inanimate object, the only personality that she can have been one that Five attributes to her. The parasocial relationship that Five creates with Delores is what drives his perseverance to continue. While the relationship may not seem "real" to an outsider looking in, the emotions that Five attributes to this relationship very much are.

Throughout his storyline, Five finds ways to enforce his parasocial relationship with Delores by projecting a personality onto her. He is often seen with her in perceived social situations, like imbibing. In turn, the Hargreeves children and other characters notice that Five treats her like a loved one. For example, there are scenes during the apocalypse where Five is sharing a drink with Delores reminiscing about a mansion and how a wine cellar was untouched. It's moments like this that demonstrate through Five's dialogue and scenery cues (Five and Delores with wine glasses in their proximity) that show their common interests. Delores is also often shown as wearing different clothing that is considered in season. Moreover, as relationships grow, so do people see patterns of behavior of their significant other. In a one-sided dialogue, Five admits that Delores thinks Apocalypse Five drinks too much. While the last example would likely have everything to do with social isolation for 40 years, many of the other perceived attributes that a viewer bestows on a persona aligns with findings in PSR literature. Since a viewer cannot examine the entire personality of an on- screen persona, there are gaps in what is known, and what is perceived. Viewers (much like Five) fill in those gaps with examples that they have witnessed as well as projections that they think a persona would act. And while Delores's entire existence is derived from Five's imagination, the characteristics that are attributed are also similar to PSR in real life.

Five is clearly attached to her, and perhaps more important than his love for her, is the fear of losing her. We know that parasocial relationships mirror social relationships when it comes to the expression of emotion. And, as mentioned earlier, parasocial breakups are part of that experience. Five is no exception to these feelings. Luther uses Delores as leverage when Five announces a plot to kill Milton Green. Five is upset at the prospect, and when Luther does drop Delores out the window, Five warps to save her. Even though Delores carries no sentience, Five's shows great determination to save her from falling.

However, with any breakup, there will be a time to let go. Viewers might see a character die, or a show ending. These breakups can bring real emotions that are similar to the Kubler Ross's Stages of Grief[20]. Almost all people will come to accept at some point that a character or a show is no longer. Once again, Five is no exception to this finding. Five delivers Delores back to the department store. On his way out, he asks an employee to give her something nice to wear. Five then gives another persona attribute to Delores saying "she likes sequins". This dramatic scene in the series demonstrates Five's acceptance of the finality of their relationship[21].

Interestingly, the heartfelt scenes and sincere emotions that Five expresses towards Delores embodies another interesting phenomenon. Umbrella Academy frames a desperate situation for Five, but also demonstrates a seemingly loving relationship. In turn, fans not only see this as a viable relationship in the show, but also take the time as a fandom to support it.

WHY WE LOVE TO LOVE THEM IDENTIFYING WITH FIVE AND HIS RELATIONSHIP WITH DELORES

While Five and Delores's relationship maintains popularity amongst Umbrella Academy fans[20], it is also one of the most interesting examples for media studies scholars to explore parasocial relationships and shipping fandom because of the fact that Delores is an inanimate object. Even with blank slate protagonists (i.e., a character that a player can project themselves onto by means of customizing name, dialogue choice, and sometimes appearance) we tend to have options with regards to how a player wants their protagonist to react. In the case of Delores, fans do not have that kind of agency. Furthermore, while we, as fans, can analyze Five's personality, temperament, communication style, and goals, we cannot do that for Delores. So how is it that we not only have a parasocial relationship with Delores but fully support Fives' meta-parasocial relationship with her? The answer lies with Five.

We, as fans, see his relationship with Delores through the lens of his own parasocial relationship with her. In the case of Five and the Umbrella Academy, the only frame of reference concerning Delores is how Five describes her. With the case of Five and Delores, viewers cannot interpret any personality beyond what Five instructs other characters about her and their relationship. As such, his relationship with her (and how fans perceive it) is the bridge and in many ways becomes an extension of how we identify with Five's and his identity.

Delores's identity is completely constructed by Five, we perceive their relationship as simply an extension of how we feel *about him*. Five consistently acts as the most pragmatic voice within the family. On a number of occasions, Five reels back the rest of the Hargreeve's children when it comes to the severity of the end of the world. While many are focused on their own respective love interests (e.g. Allison, Diego), want to resolve unfinished business, or are just nowhere to be found (Klaus), viewers can see that Five's motives are very focused. Five is constantly seen as "herding cats" with the rest of his siblings at times, which it becomes all the more apparent why his attitude and demeanor are present as they are. Furthermore, Five always appears deeply passionate about Delores. While Five keeps an otherwise "no nonsense" approach towards the end of the world, some of that rationale dissipates when other members of the Umbrella Academy mess with his affection towards Delores. After more than four decades of wandering the world alone, many fans feel sympathy with Five as that she is the one thing that held him together all that time. It is not surprising then, that many viewers of the show cheer for when we Five accomplishes his goals and sympathizes when he speaks about the only thing that elicits an emotional reaction.

His interactions with her give us insight into his insecurities and self-awareness as we are privy to their private conversations. Throughout the show, we see Five confide in Delores about his own troubles with alcoholism, ambivalence with his sibling's feelings, his negativity, and even self-reflection with Five and his mother. Delores acts as a bit of a superego to Five. While Five has his job of survival and later as an assassin, which represent two jobs allowing him a very small set of rules revolving around staying alive. He his only impeded by environmental and occupational limitations. Even then, Five still does mostly what he wants for the greater good of saving the world. However, Five's parasocial relationship with Delores is predicated around his own personal faults. Five's conversations with Delores repeatedly revolve around Five "drinking too much" (S1, E4). Five also uses Delores as a springboard for ideas, implying that Five should have a plan regarding the world ending in 6 days (S1, E4) Through these interactions, we, as viewers, are able to learn more and potentially identify more closely with Five as a character.

With that identification comes a sense of protection. Five rarely shows his soft side to fans and his siblings, given his lonely and difficult time in the midst of the apocalypse. He is often sarcastic or very serious any particular situation at hand. In fact, the only time we see Five show genuine care, concern, and love is when Delores is brought up in conversation or he describes her. Episode nine of Season one is a particularly strong indicator, not only because that's when Five says goodbye to Delores, but his dialogue conveys another reason why we enjoy the couple. As Five says goodbye, he sets Delores back in her spot in the department store, and tells her that they both get a chance at a second life. This line implies that Five deserves to move on from his life away from the apocalypse and his work as an assassin, but that he cares for Delores that she deserves her own life as well. Since their relationship was built completely out of Five's necessity for any sort of human contact, it's only fair Five sees Delores live out a life that she can choose. This changes his demeanor as she is seen as the only one that stood with him during that time of the apocalypse. It appears that Five demonstrates that Delores has empathy for him, and maybe the only one that is allowed to have empathy given the catastrophic circumstances. After Five's monologue, Five indicates that Delores tells him "he has a lot of growing up to do", emphasizing that if he is going to have his own life, he needs to reflect on his own moral compass and show compassion to others. Again, this shows Five's vulnerable side and gives fans a window into a softer side of the character.

Fans do want those characters who they feel parasocial bonds with to succeed with their endeavors[21]. Therefore, it is only natural that viewers want Five to succeed in preventing the apocalypse. This extends to Five and Delores's relationship. What's interesting about Five's case study is that despite the fact that Five is introduced to other people, his intensity with relationship with Delores remains constant and strong. The care and concern that Five shows when others threaten or mock the relationship is noticeable. While people might not identify holding those feelings with an inanimate object, they know that Five doesn't see her that way, and thus fans endorse the relationship and Five's feelings. Because we see Five's vulnerable side through his love and interactions with Delores, we root for the success of their relationship.

This so-called "meta parasocial relationship", with viewers bridging through Five to form a relationship with Delores, makes for a unique (albeit complicated) case study. The reason that fans ultimately support it as much as they do is because Five made it so. As much as Five can be an enjoyable character, his experience with his profession, his constant need for survival, and his lack of human interaction means that he emphasizes his priorities above anyone else. Delores acts as that figure to keep Five's blunt responses in check. Five's relationshp with Delores because an act of care, which eventually leads to his own realization that he can ask for help. As viewers, we root for this relationship because we want Five to succeed in his mission, and ultimately cherish the other relationships he has with the ones he cares about.

CONCLUDING THOUGHTS

Throughout *The Umbrella Academy*, there are themes of complicated relationships, loneliness, and the challenges for who people let into their weird little lives. This series not only addresses many social issues of the past and the present, but it also tackles the aspect of what it means to be human. The Hargreeves have to reconcile with this dilemma constantly, as their father seems almost more robotic and uncaring than their robot mother. The same can be said for Delores and how fans perceive the relationship between her and Five. While viewers can only see Delores's identity through Five's eyes, it's because of this fact that we can actually see Five's internal conflicts. Not only are fans told about her personality, strengths, style, and vices, she is also the one that was able to bring out emotion and love out of Five. It is also interesting that of all the human interaction that Five had with his father, siblings, and colleagues, it was a mannequin named Delores that was the most human to him. In turn, despite the fact that Delores is an object, Five's love and treatment represented that she was not an object.

NOTES

1. Cohen E. L., Hoffner C. (2016). Finding meaning in a celebrity's death: The relationshipbetween parasocial attachment, grief, and sharing educational health information related to Robin Williams on social network sites. *Computers in Human Behavior, 65,* 643–650. https://doi.org/10.1016/j.chb.2016.06.042

2. Daniel E.S. & Westerman, D. (2017). Valar morghulis (all parasocial men must die):Having nonfictional responses to a fictional character. *Communication Research Reports. 34*(2), 143-152. http://dx.doi.org/10.1080/08824096.2017.1285757

3. Eyal, K., & Dailey, R. (2012). Examining relationship maintenance in parasocial relationships.*Mass Communication and Society, 15,* 758-781.

4. Nordlund, J. (1978). Media interaction. *Communication Research,* 5, 150–175.

5. Horton, D. & Wohl, R. (1956). Mass communication and para-social interaction. *Psychiatry,* 19,215–229.

6. Levy, M. (1979), Watching TV news as para-social interaction. *Journal of Broadcasting,* 23, 69–80.

7. Noble, G. (1975). *Children in Front of the Small Screen.* Beverly Hills, Calif.: Sage

8. Honeycutt, J. (2003). *Imagined Interactions: Daydreaming About Communication.* Cresskill,NJ:Hampton Press.

9. Giles, D. (2002). Parasocial interaction: A review of the literature and a model for futureresearch. *Media Psychology,* 4, 279–305.

10. Cohen, J. (1999). Favorite characters of teenage viewers of Israeli serials. *Journal ofBroadcasting and Electronic Media,* 43, 327–345.

11. Cohen, J. (2003). Parasocial breakups: Measuring individual differences in responses to thedissolution of parasocial relationships. *Mass Communication & Society,* 6, 191–202.

12. Eyal, K., & Cohen, J. (2006). When good friends say goodbye: A parasocial breakup study. *Journal of Broadcasting & Electronic Media,* 50(3), 502-523.

13. Daniel E.S. & Westerman, D. (2017). Valar morghulis (all parasocial men must die):Having nonfictional responses to a fictional character. *Communication Research Reports.*

34(2), 143-152. http://dx.doi.org/10.1080/08824096.2017.
1285757

14. Lather, J., & Moyer-Guse, E. (2011). How do we react
when our favorite characters are taken away? An
examination of a temporary parasocial breakup. *Mass
Communication and Society, 14*(2), 196-215.

15. Tian, Q., & Hoffner, C. A. (2010). Parasocial interaction
with liked, neutral, and disliked characters on a popular
TV series. *Mass Communication and Society, 13*(3), 250-
269.

16. Cohen, J. (2003). Parasocial breakups: Measuring
individual differences in responses to thedissolution of
parasocial relationships. *Mass Communication & Society,
6,* 191–202.

17. Daniel E.S. & Westerman, D. (2017). Valar Morghulis (All
Parasocial Men Must Die):Having nonfictional responses
to a fictional character. *Communication Research Reports.
34*(2), 143-152. http://dx.doi.org/10.1080/08824096.2017.
1285757

18. Daniel E.S. (2020). When Heroes become Villains:
Developing Parasocial Relationshipswith Characters and
the Expectancy Violation Meeting the Actors. In A. Bean,
E. Daniel, S. Stewart, *Integrating Geek Culture into
Therapeutic Practice: A Clinician's Guide to Geek Therapy.*
Fort Worth, TX, Leyline

19. Ferchaud, A., Orme, S., & Daniel, E.S. (2022). Morality
inside the matrix: A qualitativeexploration of gamers'
moral considerations within virtual game space. *Journal
of Gaming and Virtual Worlds*

20. Hall, C. (2022) The best relationship in the Umbrella
Academy according to fans. Looper.https://www.looper.
com/856086/the- best-relationship-in-the-umbrella-
academy-according-to-fans/

21. Hartmann, T., Stuke, D., & Daschmann, G. (2008). Positive parasocial relationships with driversaffect suspense in racing sport spectators. *Journal of Media Psychology: Theories, Methods, and Applications, 20*(1), 24–34. https://doi.org/10.1027/1864-1105.20.1.24

KLAUS THE KINDLY CULT LEADER

KELLY CHERNIN, PHD

He was initially taken in by an older woman after mysteriously appearing. His followers believed he had supernatural insights and were blindly devoted to his teachings. He preyed on those seeking guidance, desperate to find meaning in their lives during the midst of the civil rights movement and the start of the Vietnam War. Disciples believed in anti-establishment views and remained relatively sequestered from the rest of society, only following the movements of the leader who disseminated pearls of wisdom. Even as his beliefs and guidance became more erratic, his followers remained devoutly loyal. While this paragraph could describe an infamous cult leader like Charles Manson or David Koresh, this description is a good portion of Klaus' narrative arc that plays out during Season 2 of *The Umbrella Academy*.

Klaus Hargreeves, also known as Séance, is #4 of the Hargreeves six superhero siblings. He is often portrayed as the comic relief or source of optimism for the group and could be described as the peacemaker who tries to keep the family together. His unique ability to talk to the dead not only brings him great anxiety (which he self-mediates with the use of drugs and alcohol) but also gives him a unique power to gain the adoration and, eventually cult following, of others.

Klaus is also his family's connector, a role that requires qualities not dissimilar to individuals that amass cult-like followings. However, unlike many real cult leaders, Klaus eventually grows tired of the attention and burdens associated with devout leadership and eventually leaves to return to his family[1]. Klaus' depiction as a cult leader, unlike those of the popular documentaries depicting real cults, is generally endearing and helps to further the plot of the show, but how can this cult portrayal help viewers better empathize with the nonfictional portrayals of cult members that are also popular?

While Klaus' power is primarily a source of anxiety for him in Season 1, in Season 2 of *The Umbrella Academy* we see him use it to, somewhat accidently, amass a cult following. While it is hard to define a cult, especially as the word has come to describe various elements in popular culture, there are criteria experts use to determine whether an organization may engage in what would be deemed cult-like behavior. The most significant of these features being "an organized group or solitary person whose purpose is to dominate cult members by using psychological manipulation and pressure strategies"[2] . Mass media portrayals of cult leaders tend to promote the myth that the leaders of these movements are charismatic and have supernatural persuasive powers[3], not too dissimilar to Klaus, who possesses actual powers that help him amass followers. However, a second myth often perpetuated by mass media portrayals of cults showcases the passively brainwashed follower. These myths, also loosely maintained by Klaus' cult, became common understandings of cults in the 1960s and 1970s as parents were trying to understand why their children were joining new religious movements. Those who join these fringe groups do not see themselves as joining a cult, but rather following a new movement of spiritual belonging and practice that is often taught by a particular individual with profound and innovative insights. [4] While the portrayal of Klaus' cult in *The Umbrella Academy* reinforces many of the popular myths about cults, and plays into many of the pejorative stereotypes of these groups, it also offers a more realistic version of cult membership by humanizing Klaus and giving his followers some sense of agency.

Now before we dive in, it is important to clarify what we are talking about the framing we will be using throughout this chapter to discuss, and reflect upon, cults. As the focus here is the way in which cults are portrayed in *The Umbrella Academy*, and the ways in which we watch and comprehend media centers on how audiences interpret the media they watch, we will be using the term "cult" to reflect the audience perspective of these groups, as opposed to how these communities are discussed in academic scholarship. Hopefully, this perspective will also aid in shifting away from the negative associations surrounding calling various organizations cults and towards and understanding of these groups as a community of like-minded individuals that follow a particular teaching or guru[5].

WHY ARE WE FASCINATED BY CULTS (AND ARE WE ALL CULTISTS)?

The current media environment is awash with cult documentaries – from HBO's *The Vow, which is* about the NXIVM cult, to Netflix's *Keep Sweet: Pray and Obey,* an exploration of Warren Jeffs' Fundamentalist Church of Jesus Christ of Latter-Day Saints. It is not an uncommon experience to watch these documentaries and think how we, ourselves, could "never fall prey to a cult leader's charm". That is because it is often difficult to empathize with the followers and forget that these individuals have their own agency beyond the manipulation shown in these kinds of documentaries. While we might not want to believe we are as susceptible as the cult followers in the real documentaries we view, the reality is that humans have an inherent drive to seek social and spiritual connection to fulfill our desire for belonging and purpose. To put another way, as humans, we are 'cultish' by nature[6] [7] [8] [9]. For most of us it may not look like joining a religious cult, but it could, instead, look like joining a cultish gym craze like CrossFit[10], following a problematic social media influencer, or getting a little too attached to a fictional character or a larger media fandom.

While cult-related media and content is having a moment, the fascination and stigmatization around cults is nothing new. The initial wave of our cultural fascination with cults in the United States occurred during the 1970s, and reached its peak with widespread media attention surrounding the mass murder incident in Jonestown (The Peoples Temple cult led by Jim Jones) in 1978. The second surge emerged during the 1990s, marked by extensive media coverage of the mass suicide/murder involving Heaven's Gate members (led by Marshall Applewhite)[11]. Both events were widely broadcast on national television and individuals were left with the impression that groups who prioritized communal living outside of standard societal norms and had strange beliefs were abhorrent[12].

After the events of Jonestown, parents began encouraging government organizations to do something to prevent New Religious Movements (NRMs) (or cults as they are commonly referred to by popular press), from corrupting their children. These parents viewed Jonestown as a government failure to protect citizens from manipulation and problematic ideas[13]. Given that many of these parents also belonged to their own religious organizations, generally considered traditional religious institutions, the connection to Satanism and membership in NRMs became a target for these parental groups which led to the rise of the Satanic panic of the 1980s and 1990s. The movement was highly influential and used popular daytime talk shows to spread fear and panic surrounding anything that "targeted things that threatened the Christian idea" 14,15 . For example, as part of this movement, role playing games like Dungeons and Dragons were targeted in addition to perceived fringe fandoms like interest in heavy metal music[16]. While these genres are popular today, this stigmatization of fringe fan culture is still pervasive. Even though fans of role-playing games are no longer considered to be partaking in Satanic worship, the media stigmatization of alternative lifestyles and collective living are still widely negatively portrayed today. Positive depictions of benign fringe groups in the media remain infrequent, making the portrayal of Klaus' cult in Season 2 a rare instance. While the depiction of Klaus' cult is also not realistic and tends to focus on the followers as background characters, the more lighthearted portrayal of these individuals does make them more relatable than the individuals in the "real" cults we often see in documentaries and news accounts. Klaus also acknowledges the prevalence of these groups within our society when he jokingly states, "It was the 60s, everyone had one" (S3, E8).

WHY IS KLAUS' A CULT LEADER WE'D WANT TO FOLLOW?

Klaus' portrayal of a charismatic leader in the second season of *The Umbrella Academy* provides a unique humanization of cult leaders and followers through its narrative engagement and a form of perspective taking. Throughout the first season, *The Umbrella Academy* viewers get to know Klaus, a fan favorite character[17]. Klaus cares deeply about his family, has an amusing sense of confidence, and is open to exploring his own emotions and sexuality. He is relatable to a variety of viewers and, as such, grants the audience the potential to formulate a strong attachment (or parasocial relationship with the character, for more on that see Chapters 5 and 6 in this volume). When we reunite with Klaus in Season 2, he is the leader of a cult called Destiny's Children which is an "alternative spiritual community" rooted in nature, music, drug use, and casual sex (or, as it is described by one of his followers "the holy union of our multiple spirits" [S2, E3]). Klaus is the charismatic guru of this community which is stereotypically reminiscent of the free-spirited, open love ideologies associated with hippies and communes of the 1960s. He is worshiped in almost a religious way as he preaches love and peace to his followers.

Unlike the rightly villainized portrayals of Keith Raniere, the leader of NXIVM or Warren Jeffs, (the leader of a polygamous group that facilitated the sexual abuse of underaged girls), Klaus' motivates with love and kindness. There is little to no depictions of Klaus manipulating his followers in ways we often see utilized by the cult leaders portrayed in popular documentaries. Instead, we see Klaus reciting song lyrics from the songs of our time and Alcoholics Anonymous self-help steps to his cult followers and thus can also see ourselves as willing disciples of his pop culture mantras.

However, it is worth pointing out that parts of Klaus' story arc in Season 2 does adhere to the mass media portrayals we often see from the cult leader portrayals in popular documentaries. After being thrust into the year 1960, Klaus uses his charm to convince a rich woman to take care of him after getting kicked out of a diner for his unseemly appearance and odor. This narrative plot is like that of David Koresh, the leader of the Branch Davidians. Koresh originally gained favor with Lois Roden, the widow of the group's former leader who was in her late 60s[18]. Like many real cult leaders (i.e. Keith Raniere, Jim Jones, Sun Myung Moon) who seek international followers and philosophies to grow their influence, Klaus also travels to Mexico and India in subsequent years growing his following.

While the viewer is meant to believe that Klaus is following the trajectory of real cult leaders, Klaus is not portrayed in the same manipulative way. Fans of the show find Klaus endearing because he has a relatable back story. While the other Hargreeves siblings are vigilante crime fighters, live on the moon, or a famous movie star, Klaus is a drug addict alcoholic who is just trying to get through the day[19]. Klaus is also charismatic and often serves as the comic relief during family tension and thus the show[20]. In a Reddit thread devoted to *The Umbrella Academy*, users shared their opinion on Klaus stating things like "I love him. You can tell he loves his family —he often acts the peacekeeper at his own expense." These perspectives help to showcase Klaus' charm not only as a character in a show, but as a potential figure to admire in general.

CHANGING THE WAY WE THINK ABOUT CULTS

Exposure states is a term used to explain the degree to which we are paying attention and processing the media we are watching[21]. These states are attentional, automatic, transported, and self-reflexive[22]. These states help us understand why the more we are concentrating on a show, the more likely they are to develop a strong attachment to a character or get emotionally invested in a plot.

In the past, media effects literature tended to assume that most people were highly susceptible to media's influence. However, as recent literature suggests, the influence may be more limited23,24. Someone watching *The Umbrella Academy* is not likely to join a cult because they liked Klaus. Similarly, that same individual will probably not join a cult because they watched a documentary about David Koresh. While the effect of watching these programs is not going to be extreme enough to directly lead to cult membership or aversion, it may at least be subtle enough to build a sense of empathy depending on the exposure state of viewers[25][26].

During the attentional state, individuals generally have a high degree of concentration; they are aware of the message. As noted above, this is the state early media effects research assumed was taking place because participants were often watching media in controlled lab environments[27]. In reality, individuals are likely consuming media in an automatic state where messages are processed "automatically in an unconscious manner"[28]. In this context, individuals are processing media messages without conscious awareness or deliberate thought. We are often distracted while we are watching our favorite shows like *The Umbrella Academy* and likely scrolling on a phone, or we are possibly distracted by something that happened earlier at work.

While it is difficult to measure exposure during an automatic state, it is still relevant considering this is how many individuals consume media. Cultivation theory, or the idea that the more individuals consume a certain type of media the more they believe that to be true of reality (e.g., those who watch crime shows believe that there is more crime in the world than there really is), assumes that people are watching in an automatic state29,30,31. Based on this idea people who watch cult documentaries, may be more likely to harbor negative perceptions of not only the pervasiveness of cults, but may also garner more judgement toward those who would join one. In a sense, *The Umbrella Academy* could possibly serve as an anecdote to the negative perception viewers may hold if they also consume non-fictional cult documentaries[32].

Given the popularity of the cult genre documentary and shows like *The Umbrella Academy,* there is a good chance that while most viewers are probably consuming media in an automatic state, there are some that are in a transported and even self-reflexive state. Considering the abundance of fan pages and merchandise dedicated to *The Umbrella Academy*, one can reasonably infer that these individuals are actively interacting with the content. However, even those who are watching in a more passive, automatic state are still likely to become more aware of the emotions and justifications those in cults, whether fictional or nonfictional, experience.

While one hopes that viewers watching any of these shows in automatic states will be more receptive to empathic emotions toward cult followers, there is more promise for those who watch these shows in a transported or self-reflexive state. In a transported state, audience members feel like they are a part of the world created by the show[33]. Show creators build these worlds to mirror real world experiences through sets, costumes, locations, plots, characters, etc. The idea is to get the audience to feel involved and connected; to be a part of the story. *The Best of Klaus from The Umbrella Academy Season 2* YouTube page has over 10,000 likes and has been viewed 307,000 times[34]. Given these numbers, it is clear that fans feel connected to Klaus. The fact that viewers are watching supplemental material on sites other than Netflix could demonstrate that they have viewed the program in a transported state. Viewers feel connected to the character and want to engage with the content beyond watching regular episodes. In a transportive state, "what is common is the notion that individuals escape to the fictional world and have limited contact or attention to the real world"[35] Viewing additional content online thus suggests that these individuals want to continue feeling connected to these fictional worlds.

While the viewers' immediate connection with Klaus is likely the result of a parasocial relationship (discussed in more detail later in this chapter) rather than a transported state of viewing, *The Umbrella Academy* possesses the capacity to captivate the audience with its message, fostering deeper character connections and empathy[36]. Narrative transportation requires a connection with the characters and thus has the ability to foster empathetic feelings. The more people connect with characters, the more likely they are to engage with perspective taking. In this state, people are less likely to feel like they are being persuaded and are more likely to mirror the beliefs and attitudes of the characters they feel connected to; therefore, they are in a more heightened state of perspective-taking, which can build empathy for groups different than the viewer[37]. In theory, individuals who were in a transported state while watching Season 2 of *The Umbrella Academy* could understand more why someone would be enthralled by a charismatic guru like Keith Ranieri because they could relate to the individuals who followed Klaus and saw him as enlightening. The connection viewers build with Klaus may prompt a more accepting position for why an individual may be inclined to follow someone who has a different way of thinking.

Finally, in a self-reflexive state, "people are not only consciously aware of the elements in the message; they are also aware of the processing of those elements"[38]. Considering the reflective nature linked to this state, viewers may find themselves delving deeper into the reasons behind the popularity of cult documentaries or the motivations driving someone to join Klaus' cult, extending beyond the mere influence of a parasocial relationship. In this state, viewers are more likely to unpack some of the problematic and stigmatizing views the cult documentary genre perpetuates. While understanding these exposure states is key to determining how someone watching *The Umbrella Academy* would be more empathetic to the cult followers in non-fictional documentaries, it is also important to understand the connection *The Umbrella Academy* viewers may have to Klaus through parasocial relationships.

CONNECTING WITH KLAUS: PARASOCIAL RELATIONSHIPS

As mentioned above, our parasocial relationship with Klaus is likely what underlies our attachment to Klaus as a character and, consequently, a cult leader. Parasocial relationships (PSRs) are one-sided attachments that individuals have with either a celebrity or media figure. These relationships can also be with fictional characters. The way cult documentaries are structured, it is unlikely that the audience is going to build a parasocial relationship with the characters portrayed. While not all cult leaders possess these qualities, the cult-leaders depicted in popular documentaries tend to be masochistic, oversee – if not participate in – abuse of their followers, show little remorse for their actions, and lack empathy[39]. Keith Ranieri convinced his "girlfriends" to have other female followers of NXIVM brand themselves with his initials and starve themselves, so they fit an ideal view of beauty that Ranieri preferred[40].

These real-life cult leaders are portrayed as monsters and exploiters and justifiably so. Even though real-world cult leaders we see in popular documentaries tend to abuse their followers, the documentation of how they amassed their following in the first place tends to be overlooked. That is, it tends to gloss over the fact that cult leaders are charismatic leaders that quite literally lead people down a path of perceived certainty when times see uncertain. For example, NXIVM was originally sold as a self-empowerment program. Followers were asked to confront their emotional triggers in a way that was supposed to promote a more optimistic lifestyle[41].

However, when we watch cult documentaries, the positive elements of these groups are eliminated or buried. While there is some discussion of the sense of community that was felt or the importance of feeling a sense of belonging , the scenes are edited in a way that "dive deep into the stories of real people committing acts that are sometimes so twisted and heinous, they seem stranger (and certainly more gruesome) than fiction"[42]. Although there are some exceptions, the followers are portrayed as lost souls who were easily manipulated by a monster.

With Klaus, the viewer can see his progression as a cult leader. How he amassed more followers using his charm and supernatural abilities. He uses his knowledge of the future to seem forward thinking and wise. Klaus is also likely taking advantage of his followers in other ways by receiving gifts—his cult resides in an opulent mansion—and sexual favors (though the only romantic interaction we see with Klaus and a follower is when Ben possesses Klaus so he can be with someone he felt a genuine connection with). Like many real cult leaders, Klaus uses his knowledge of the end of the world from the first season to convince his followers to prepare for this inevitable doom. While Klaus' end of the world is "real" in the sense that it is part of *The Umbrella Academy* plot, real cult leaders (i.e. William Miller of the Millerites, Jim Jones, David Koresh, Marshal Applewhite, and Aum Shinrikyo) used similar apocalyptic predictions to gain followers[43]. In addition, he uses future song lyrics like "don't go chasing waterfalls" in a way that comes off as sage advice. The viewer gets to see the relational progression and understand why someone would follow Klaus beyond just the parasocial relationship a viewer may have built with him from the first season. These traits that are considered disturbing when viewed in the context of real cult leaders are endearing to those who are fans of Klaus. This is likely more emphasized in *The Umbrella Academy* because Klaus is not depicted as lying to and abusing his followers.

In Klaus' case, the end of the world is not a lie, and he expresses this when Five claims that the end of the world is now going to happen sooner stating "Oh my god, my cult is going to be so pissed. Five, I told them we had until 2019." This demonstrates that Klaus does care about his followers.

It is also worth pointing out that parasocial relationships can significantly influence viewers' behavior. In the case of Klaus fans, this has the potential to sway behavior positively in the sense that it can build understanding and awareness for real life followers, but it is unlikely to cause harm in the opposite direction since individuals are less likely to have a stronger connection with fictional characters that they dislike[44]. In addition, audiences are more likely to empathize with the characters they build these relationships with[45]. The connection to PSRs and empathy are key to understanding why a show like *The Umbrella Academy* could help to build more acceptance for actual cult followers and more awareness that we are all susceptible to joining one of these groups.

To begin, parasocial relationships can be constructive for those who have them[46]. Individuals who identify as having these kinds of relationships with specific characters are report experience greater empathy toward them, leading to a heightened understanding of others' emotions and an improved ability to relate to their feelings[47]. Viewers can connect with Klaus' personal journey and the way he discovered purpose as a cult leader. Fans can appreciate Klaus' growth, thanks to their insights into the show's plot and character development. Once more, fans witnesss a favorable portrayal of a cult leader, offering them insight into why someone in a real-life scenario might be initially attracted to a cult.

IMPORTANT DISTINCTIONS AND HEALTHIER MEDIA PORTRAYALS

Although the parasocial relationship between that of fan and character and the one between cult member and guru may share some similarities, there are important distinctions between the two. The one-sided relationship with Klaus is one-sided not because he does not reciprocate feelings, but rather because he is in a fictional/imaginative world. The one-sided relationship with the guru or cult leader is because that individual likely harbors manipulative, narcissistic tendencies. Many actual gurus want you to be near them so they can control you; they use physical and emotional proximity as ways to manipulate followers[48]. By the time Klaus meets up with the rest of his siblings, Klaus is trying to avoid his flock. He wants to be by himself or with his family; not feel burdened by the pressures of leading—power a real cult leader would relish in. While some accuse Klaus of being a narcissist, he is actually quite caring and willing to listen to criticism from others in a way that helps him emotionally grow. Klaus' most troubling behaviors in Season 2 are countered by having Ben around as his conscience and sounding board. Klaus also cares deeply about saving Dave, his love interest from Season 1.

Klaus can be over the top, but unlike real cult leaders, he does not bolster his sense of importance in a way that puts others in danger. Given the events of Season 1, Klaus was aware that the end of the world was coming and in a way was giving his followers a sense of community before that time arrived. Unlike real cult leaders, this was not a delusional prophecy disseminated to gain power. Klaus' goal was also not to stifle dissent or pit members against each other[49]. Generally, Klaus was just depicted as performing supernatural acts with the help of Ben's ghost or giving out advice that was somewhat insightful. Never once was Klaus depicted doing something that would potentially endanger those who followed him. It should be noted that there are cults that would also be considered somewhat benevolent, like the Hare Krishnas, but these are not the movements that become the subject of popular cult documentaries or the major media stories like the Jonestown murders, the standoff in Waco with the Branch Davidians, or the far-right Christian movements that boast members like the Duggar family.

In addition to a lack of harm, another healthier depiction of

Klaus' cult was the use of more positive emotions to draw in the audience and members. Normal cults and even the depiction of cults tend to use fear as a driving force. The popularity of the true crime genre, of which cult documentaries are a subgenre, tend to sensationalize violence, coercion, and fear. "The media's portrayal of criminal justice-related issues is important because the media affect consumers' perceptions about key issues[50]. Again, the news coverage and documentaries that depict real cults tend to focus on violence, fear, and manipulation. The tactics that cult leaders use to manipulate followers are understandably framed in a negative light, but this makes it difficult for the average viewer to understand why a seemingly average person would join these groups. Newer documentaries like *The Vow* and other documentaries associated with the NXIVM cult do a little better at depicting former followers in a positive light, but these followers also tend to come from white, wealthy backgrounds, a group that garners more sympathetic media portrayals naturally (e.g., why we have more news coverage of missing white women than of POC and indigenous women)[51]. The portrayal of cults and their leaders in a more negative light tends to heighten stigmatization, or at the very least, amplify the voyeuristic fascination linked to former cult members. Klaus, however, was never portrayed in a negative light. His rise to cult power is framed as a humorous montage. While many socially consciousness campaigns use fear tactics or negative emotions to try to change behavior (e.g., climate change and showing the destruction of the environment), using positive emotions are actually more likely to persuade people to change their behavior[52]. Therefore, if the goal is to use media to create more empathy and understanding, then more humorous, positive portrayals of cults like Klaus' cult are more likely to help educate people about the signs of cult indoctrination than those that use fear tactics. At the very least, these positive portrayals of cults or any NRM does help to reframe some of the stigmatization propagated by negative past media portrayals.

People who join cults tend to have higher educations and more open-minded views[53]. They are often people that are seeking guidance or a sense of community. Anyone is susceptible to joining a cult. When watching a documentary about cults, it can be easy to assume that one is above the manipulation tactics used by Keith Raniere or Jim Jones. However, the more one thinks they are less likely to be persuaded by messages, the more overconfidence they have in their abilities to discern problematic behaviors and socially undesirable messages[54]. A comedic and more emotionally complex portrayal of a cult, such as Klaus' storyline in season two of *The Umbrella Academy,* possesses the power to immerse fans in a world that is characterized by greater empathy and emotional depth. It creates a realm where viewers can foster greater understanding and compassion for individuals who have become involved in cults and are attempting to rebuild their lives after undergoing a traumatic experience. Klaus serves as the compassionate cult leader who enriches the experience of media consumption with a deeper sense of empathy.

NOTES

1. McKeown, J. (Writer) & Surjik, S. (2020, July 31). The Swedish job (Season, 2, Episode 3) [TV series episode]. In. G. Way, G. Ba, and J. Slater (Executive Producers), The Umbrella Academy. Netflix
2. Rousselet, M., O. Duretete, J.B. Hardouin, and M. Grall-Bronnec. (2017). "Cult Membership: What Factors Contribute to Joining or Leaving?" *Psychiatry Research* 257 (November): 27–33. doi:10.1016/ j.psychres.2017.07.018.
3. Richardson, J. T. (2021). "The Myth of the Omnipotent Leader: The Social Construction of a Misleading Account of Leadership in New Religious Movements." *Nova Religio* 24 (4): 11–25. doi:10.1525/ nr.2021.24.4.11.
4. Baker, E. (1989). *New Religious Movements: A Practical Introduction.* HMSO.

5. Barrett, D. V. (2001). *The New Believers: A Survey of Sects, Cults and Alternative Religions.* Cassell & Co.

6. Montell, A. (2021). *Cultish:The Language of Fanaticism.* Harper Collins.

7. Gilbert, S. (2021). We choose our cults every day. *The Atlantic. https://www.theatlantic.com/culture/archive/2021/06/review-cultish- amanda-montell-language-fanaticism/619165/*

8. Ganguly, T. (2018). Connecting Their Selves: The Discourse of Karma, Calling, and Surrendering among Western Spiritual Practitioners in India. *Journal of the American Academy of Religion, 86*(4), 1014–1045. https://doi-org.proxy006.nclive.org/10.1093/jaarel/lfy015

9. Jacquez, F., Vaughn, L. M., & Hardy-Besaw, J. (2024). Immigrant Perspectives of Social Connection in a Nontraditional Migration Area. *Healthcare (2227-9032), 12*(6), 686. https://doi-org.proxy006.nclive.org/10.3390/healthcare12060686

10. Weathers, C. (2022, October 22). CrossFit is a cult: Why so many of its defenders are so defensive. *Salon.* Retrieved from https://www.salon.com/2014/10/22/crossfit_is_a_cult_why_so_many_of_its_defender-s_are_so_defensi ve_partner/

11. Lucas, P. C., & Robbins, T. (2004). *New Religious Movements in The Twenty-First Century: Legal, Political, and Social Challenges in Global Perspective.* Routledge.

12. Fenick, B. (2020). A culture of fear: Religious panic and modern society. [Unpublished honors thesis]. UNC Pembroke.

13. Lucas, P. C., & Robbins, T. (2004). *New Religious Movements in The Twenty-First Century: Legal, Political, and Social Challenges in Global Perspective.* Routledge.

14. Huges, S. (2017). American monsters: Tabloid media and

the satanic panic, 1970-2000. *Journal of American Studies, 51*(3), 303-319.

15. Fenick, B. (2020). A culture of fear: Religious panic and modern society. [Unpublished honors thesis]. UNC Pembroke.

16. Laycock, J. (2015). Dangerous Games: What the Moral Panic Over Role-Playing Games Says About Play, Religion, and Imagined Worlds. University of California Press.

17. Bruce, L. (2022, Dec 4). Why Klaus from Umbrella Academy is so powerful and loved by fans. Movieweb. https://movieweb.com/klaus-umbrella-academy-power-love/#:~:text=While other characters have relatable,average person would not experience

18. Wilson, C. (2000). *The Devil's Party: A History of Charlatan Messiahs.* Virgin Books

19. Ibid.

20. Nguyen, J. (2022, Oct. 22). 'The Umbrella Academy': 10 Times Klaus Hargreeves earned his status as "fan favorite." Collider. https://collider.com/the-umbrella-academy-times-klaus- hargreeves-earned-fan-favorite/#dancing-with-his-father-rsquo-s- ash-in-his-sister-rsquo-s-skirt-season-1-episode-1-ldquo-we-only-see-each-other-at-weddings-and-funerals-quot

21. Potter, W. J. (2009). Conceptualizing the audience. In R. L. Nabi & M. B. Oliver (Eds.), *The Sage Handbook of Media Processes and Effects.* (pp. 19-34). Sage Publications.

22. Potter, W. J. (2009). Conceptualizing the audience. In R. L. Nabi & M. B. Oliver (Eds.), *The Sage Handbook of Media Processes and Effects.* (pp. 19-34). Sage Publications.

23. Ibid.

24. Lyon, B. A. (2022). Why we should rethink the third person effect: disentangling bias and earned confidence using behavioral data. *Journal of Communication, 72*(5), 565-577. https://doi.org/10.1093/joc/jqac021

25. Ibid.

26. Bryant, J., & Oliver, M. B. (2009). *Media effects : advances in theory and research* (3rd ed.). Routledge.

27. Lyon, B. A. (2022). Why we should rethink the third person effect: disentangling bias and earned confidence using behavioral data. *Journal of Communication, 72*(5), 565-577. https://doi.org/10.1093/ joc/jqac021

28. Potter, W. J. (2009). Conceptualizing the audience. In R. L. Nabi & M. B. Oliver (Eds.), *The Sage Handbook of Media Processes and Effects.* (pp. 19-34). Sage Publications.

29. Ibid.

30. Gerbner, G. (1969). Toward "cultural indicators": The analysis of mass mediated public message systems. *AV Communication Review, 170*(2), 137-148.

31. Shrum, L. J. (1996). Psychological processes underlying cultivation effects: Further tests of construct accessibility. *Human Communication Research, 22*, 482-509.

32. Compton J (2012). "Inoculation Theory". In Dillard JP, Shen L (eds.). *The SAGE Handbook of Persuasion: Developments in Theory and Practice.* SAGE Publications. pp. 220–236.

33. Potter, W. J. (2009). Conceptualizing the audience. In R. L. Nabi & M. B. Oliver (Eds.), *The Sage Handbook of Media Processes and Effects.* (pp. 19-34). Sage Publications.

34. Netflix. (2020, Aug 8). Best of Klaus from The Umbrella Academy Season 2. YouTube. https://www.youtube.com/ watch?v=gFu9gS5IpKo

35. Warren, S. (2020). Binge-Watching as a predictor of narrative transportation using HLM. *Journal of Broadcasting & Electronic Media, 64*(2), 89-110. https:// doi-org.proxy006.nclive.org/10. 1080/08838151.2020.1718985, p. 93.

36. Green, M. C., & Brock, T. C. (2000). The role of

transportation in the persuasiveness of public narratives. *Journal of Personality and Social Psychology*, 79(5), 701.

37. Green, M. C., & Clark, J. L. (2013). Transportation into narrative worlds: implications for entertainment media influences on tobacco use. *Addiction, 108*(3), 477–484.

38. Potter, W. J. (2009). Conceptualizing the audience. In R. L. Nabi & M. B. Oliver (Eds.), *The Sage Handbook of Media Processes and Effects.* (pp. 19-34). Sage Publications. p. 27

39. Henderson, J. (2024). Psychological manipulation and Cluster-B personality traits of cult leaders [ProQuest Information & Learning]. In *Dissertation Abstracts International: Section B: The Sciences and Engineering* (Vol. 85, Issue 2–B).

40. Grigoriadis, V. (2018, May 30). Inside Nxivm, the 'sex cult' that preached empowerment. *The New York Times.* *https://www.nytimes.com/2018/05/30/magazine/sex-cult-empowerment- nxivm-keith-raniere.html#:~:text=Nxivm positioned itself as the,particularly those formed in childhood.*

41. Ibid.

42. Siclait, A., Talbert, S., Pelto, A., & Douba, R. (2023, Aug 15). 64 best true crime documentaries to stream in 2023 on Netflix, Hulu, HBO Max, and more: Because binge-watching 'Missing: The Lucie Blackman' case just wasn't enough...Woment's Health. https://www. womenshealthmag.com/life/g28068183/best-true-crime-documentaries/, para 2

43. Parker, J. L. (2011, April 5). Notorious doomsday prophets and cults. CNBC. https://www.cnbc.com/2011/04/06/ Notorious-Doomsday- Prophets-and-Cults.html

44. Tian, Q., & Hoffner, C. A. (2010). Parasocial interaction with liked, neutral, and disliked characters on a popular TV series. *Mass Communication & Society, 13*(3), 250–269. https://doi.org/10.1080/15205430903296051

45. Scherer, H., Diaz, S., Iannone, N., McCarty, M., Branch, S., and Kelly, J. (2022). "Leave Britney alone!": parasocial relationships and empathy. *The Journal of Social Psychology, 162*(1), 128-142. https//doi.org/10.1080/00224545.2021.1997889

46. Gabriel, S., Read, J. P., Young, A. F., Bachrach, R. L., & Troisi, J. D. (2017). Social surrogate use in those exposed to trauma: I get by with a little help from my (fictional) friends. *Journal of Social and Clinical Psychology, 36*(1), 41-63. https://doi.org/10.1521/jscp.2017.36.1.41

47. Davis, M. H. (1983). Measuring individual differences in empathy: Evidence for a multidimensional approach. *Journal of Personality and Social Psychology, 44*(1), 113-126. https://doi.org/10.1007/978-0-387-30715-2_20.

48. Lucia, A. (2018). Guru sex: Charisma, proxemic desire, and the haptic logics of the guru-disciple relationship. *Journal of the American Academy of Religion, 86*(4), 953-988. doi:10.1093/jaarel/lfy025

49. Neuharth, D. (2021, March 17). 9 ways many narcissists behave like cult leaders. Psychology Today. https://www.psychologytoday.com/ us/blog/narcissism-demystified/202103/9-ways-many-narcissists- behave-cult-leaders#:~:text=Individuals high in narcissism, like,with little tolerance for dissent.

50. Slakoff, D. C. (2022). The mediated portrayal of intimate partner violence in true crime podcasts: Strangulation, isolation, threats of violence, and coercive control. *Violence Against Women, 28*(6/7), 1659–1683. https://doi-org.proxy006.nclive.org/10.1177/10778012211019055, p. 1660

51. Neely, C. L. (2015). *You're Dead—So What?: Media, Police, And The Invisibility of Black Women as Victims of Homicide.* Michigan State University Press.

52. Shiota, M. N., Papies, E. K., Preston, S. D., & Sauter, D. A. (2021). Positive affect and behavior change. Current Opinion in Behavioral Sciences, 39, 222-228. https://doi. org/10.1016/ j.cobeha.2021.04.022

53. Dawson, L. L. (2006). *Comprehending Cults: The Sociology of New Religious Movements.* Oxford University Press.

54. Gunther, A. C., & Mundy, P. (1993). Biased optimism and the third- person effect. *Journalism Quarterly, 70*(1), 58-67.

REACTIONARY REACTIONS? FAN RESPONSES TO VIKTOR'S IDENTITY DEVELOPMENT

SOFIA V. RHEA AND LARAMIE D.
TAYLOR, PHD

T

he Umbrella Academy, the hit Netflix show based on comics by Gerard Way and Gabriel Bá, has seen consistent and widespread viewership since the release of its first season of episodes in February 2019[1]. Within the first month of airing, 45 million households viewed the series[2]. Viewers collectively spent 124,530,000 viewing hours during the first week of season three's release in June 2022[3].

The Umbrella Academy stands out from other mainstream super-hero narratives in its divergence from the monolithically heteronor-mative plot points typical of the genre[4]. Two key characters in the franchise are openly LGBTQ ; however, their identities are never explicitly labeled[5]. One character, in particular, develops their iden-tity as the show progresses. In the first season, the character, then known as Vanya Hargreeves, presents as a woman, uses she/her pronouns, and participates in a heterosexual relationship. In the second season, this same character, using the same name and pronouns as in season one, is in a romantic and sexual relationship with a woman. In season three, Vanya transitions to Viktor, coming out as male, at the beginning of the second episode. *The Umbrella*

Academy is unique in that fans have thus been able to see a main character explore and develop their sexual and gender identity through three distinct stages in the greater context of fantastical missions and extraordinary circumstances.

For the purposes of this chapter, we will refer to Viktor, formerly known as Vanya, as "V". In both our dataset and in the context of the show, discussions of V, including names used, are tied to the historical context of the posts as well as the show. In seasons one and two, this character identifies as a woman and uses the name Vanya. However, as the show progresses and this character's gender identity shifts, they begin to use he/him pronouns and change their name to Viktor. To avoid confusion and dead-naming this character, more general discussions of Vanya (i.e., the character as presented in season 1 or 2) or Viktor (i.e., the character as presented in season 3), particularly those that transcend seasons, will be abbreviated to "V". This also allows discussion of the same character that has a different gender identity in the television program and the comic books upon which the program is based.

In this chapter we will explore how fans react to V's identity development across multiple seasons of *The Umbrella Academy*. Using a variety of text analysis tools, we explore how and if discussions of V on Reddit shift as the character's identity develops. We examine what words are connected to discussions of V, what topics emerge across seasons, and the overall tone (positive or negative) of these discussions. Doing so allows us to determine if fan reactions and discussions surrounding V shift as the show and V's identity develop.

V'S IDENTITY DEVELOPMENT AT A GLANCE

In the first season of *The Umbrella Academy* V, then known as Vanya and presenting as a woman, is in a heterosexual relationship with a man named Leonard Peabody. Throughout the season, their relationship develops, and the viewer eventually learns that Leonard is the antagonist of the season and is using his relationship with V to instigate the apocalypse. Although V is often an uncertain, awkward relationship partner, this is presented as a natural consequence of her long-time alienation from her family; there is no overt or implied suggestion of LGBTQ identity.

V's LGBTQ identity begins to visibly develop throughout the second season of the series. As the world ends in season one, the characters are dispersed through time, and V finds herself in rural Texas of the 1960s. Here, she is taken in by a married couple with a child. V, still going by Vanya and using she/her pronouns at this time, begins a secret romantic relationship with Sissy, the woman who takes her in. The two engage in an affair for the duration of the season as both of their sexual identities develop.

During season three, we see V's expression of their gender identity begin to develop. In the second episode of this season, V cuts their hair and, when called Vanya by a sibling, corrects them: "It's, uh, Viktor". Brief confusion follows, and the sibling asks, "Who's Viktor?" "I am; it's who I've always been," is the reply. The other characters in the series immediately accept V as their brother, respecting his gender pronouns and new name, even offering to throw a party to celebrate and acknowledge the transition. Despite the familial drama and turmoil in this season, Viktor's gender identity is only brought up in ways that are loving, accepting, or supportive.

Notably, this change in gender expression is not present in the initial comic series upon which the television show is based. V's gender identity development in the series was written into the series in part as a direct response to the personal gender identity expression of Elliot Page, the actor who portrays the character. When actor Elliot Page came out as a nonbinary and transgender in 2020, the creators of the television series decided to have V's character develop along with the actor. During this time, Page became the first cast member of a television series to undergo a mid-series gender transition while maintaining a role as a regular cast member[6]. Notably, this was a conscious choice on the part of the show's creative team. They could have chosen to change actors or ask that Page continue to play the role of Vanya, a character that was not in line with Page's gender identity. Additionally, given the fantastical missions and sci-fi- rooted drama in the show, V's transition could have easily been explained away in various supernatural ways–alternative timelines, a human cloning experiment, or what have you. Instead, *The Umbrella Academy* creative team made the decision to veer away from the comics and have a main character develop their gender identity as a plot point in season three. In an interview on *The Late Show* with Seth Meyers, Page discussed the process of incorporating his gender identity journey into the show's plot, citing the support he received from *The Umbrella Academy's* showrunner, Steve Blackman, and the additional help they enlisted to ensure that Viktor's transition was incorporated into the storyline in a seamless and respectful manner[7].

The complex and eventually non-canonical development of V's identity development allows for a unique opportunity to explore how fans react to shifts in a character's identity development, especially when these shifts are not present in the original source material.

THE IMPORTANCE AND PREVALENCE OF ONLINE FAN DISCOURSE

If you are reading this book, you are probably a fan of *The Umbrella Academy*. There are many ways that we, as human, express enthusiasm, or fanship, for the things we enjoy. Fans attend conventions, create and wear costumes inspired by their fandoms, read books, watch fan media, or even write a chapter in a quasi-academic book exploring fandom. However, one of the most common ways fans experience their fanship is through discourse around the object of their fanship. This is true not only for in-person conversations but also for online discourse. In a study of *Star Trek* fans, Taylor[8] found that 28% reported discussing *Star Trek* online, and 60% reported reading *Star Trek*-related websites. The numbers were even higher for fans of fictional texts generally, with 38% reporting discussing their preferred text online and 68% looking at relevant websites. A lot of the important work of fanship occurs online, much of it on Reddit.

Reddit is a particularly popular hub for fans of televised media. In fact, Reddit has been identified as one of the top sources of information for people to find additional information about a show, actor, or character[9]. Nearly half (47%) of respondents to a recent survey said they turn to Reddit to find such information. Reddit's unique structure allows for fan community discussions to blossom and for fans to interact with one another in a mediated online setting. The platform is structured in such a way that users can join and interact in various thematically structured forums and pick and choose particular discussion threads within each of those forums. An individual fan can find other fans and engage with those who are not only interested in the same text, but the same questions, issues, or insights. Reddit is among the most popular social networking sites, consistently ranking in the top ten most popular social media sites[10]. This self-proclaimed "front page of the internet" has an extensive user base, with 430 million monthly active users[11].

FANON VS CANNON: REACTIONS TO CANONICAL INFIDELITY

One thing fans talk about a lot, especially online, is consistency. Sometimes, they discuss how little elements of the text conflict with others. But in more complex fictional universes, where there are multiple texts telling the same or overlapping stories, fans often talk about how consistency and inconsistency across different iterations of the text—is the movie like the comic book, does the show accurately reflect the books, does the remake match up with the original, and so on. Canonical or "canon" content in popular media refers to material found in the original storyline or source material of a given show, movie, or book[12], or within the subset of original narratives agreed to be authoritative by fans generally. Distinctions between original content and so- called "fanon" are integral in active fan communities, particularly ones where fanfiction is predominant. Fanon content is content that is not in the original or "canon" source material but is widely accepted by the fan community at large. Canonical storylines in popular media may include dominant relationships that are present in the original narrative, while fanonical storylines may build upon these existing storylines by hypothesizing how character relationships progressed or by extending the plot beyond the original source material. The line between fanon and canon content can grow blurry in larger fan bases with a history of established and widely-accepted fan lore.

Fans, out of commitment to the original text, can react negatively to violations of canon in adaptations of original source material. Research on this "canonical infidelity" is somewhat limited. Work exploring fan responses to Marvel Cinematic Universe (MCU) adaptations of Marvel comic books has identified fan backlash in the face of canonical infidelity[13]. For example, fans were surprised and upset to see the erasure of the canonical lesbian relationship between the characters Akena and Ayo in the film adaptation of *Black Panther*. Marvel's decision to remove the relationship between the two female warriors sparked widespread discussions on heteronormativity in superhero films and the erasure of queerness in the MCU[14]. Responses to casting choices for the 2023 live-action remake of *The Little Mermaid* have also demonstrated the varied responses that come in the face of diversions from original source material. After announcing that Ariel would be played by African American actress and singer Halle Bailey, forceful backlash ensued from predominantly white fans[15]. Angry fans coined the viral hashtag "#NotMy-Ariel", calling for Disney to reevaluate and recast the film with an actress who more closely resembled the Ariel in the original film[16]. It is interesting to note that other Disney live-action remakes of popular animated films have added new musical numbers and plot elements, also construable as canonical infidelity without engendering the same sort of oppositional reaction. It may be that fans are comfortable with story changes across media but are more concerned about canon with regard to characters.

The decision on the part of *The Umbrella Academy* showrunners to first insert a lesbian relationship for V as Vanya in Season 2, and then to respond to Elliot Page's public coming out as male by adapting V's identity from the canonical Vanya to Viktor in Season 3, represents a particular instance of canonical infidelity. Like many of those that have garnered public discussion, the actual inconsistency is relatively minor: V's powers do not change, their relationship with family members does not change (beyond the complicated familial dynamics inherent to the plot), their basic role in the story does not change. The change, as with the changes described in *Mermaid* and *Panther* above, is principally one of identity. This does not, however, mean that the change is not worthy of note; identity matters, and portrayals of underrepresented identities can matter a lot.

Research has shown that mediated contact with positively portrayed LGBTQ characters aids in prejudice reduction[17], partly because seeing LGBTQ characters often involve the development of parasocial relationships with those characters[18] (for a more about parasocial relationships, see Chapters 5 and 6 in this volume). As audience members parasocially get to know and care about LGBTQ characters, those relationships work to provide salient exemplars that inform later attitude formation and decisions. But how will fans respond when a character's sexual or gender identity changes mid-series? Some case studies have demonstrated widespread acceptance of celebrities coming out as LGBTQ, as was the case in online discussions of German international football player Thomas Hitzlsperger, who came out publicly as gay shortly after retiring from competitive play but while still involved in the world of professional soccer[19].

However, other fannish responses to questions of identity in popular culture have been less positive. The #GamerGate phenomenon, when large numbers of video game fans collectively harassed and attacked female game designers, scholars, and critics, demonstrated how online fan spaces can become "echo chambers of anger"[20] around issues of gender.

FAN REACTIONS TO V'S TRANSITION

We were curious to better understand fan dynamics around gender and sexual identity specifically in relation to Vanya/ Viktor Hargreeves. There are, of course, many ways to study and interrogate these kinds of fan discussions. Explorations of both individual and collective responses can help shed light on how fans may respond to their media of interest. Each individual's fanish experience is valid and worthy of study, but we were primarily interested in exploring the broad, general patterns of fan responses. To explore these larger patterns of fan responses, we analyzed large amounts of written text shared by fans in public forums. Our plan was to seek insight into how fans responded to V's sexuality and gender development by looking across comments in response to all three seasons of *Umbrella*. By sampling fan responses from the time of the release of all three seasons, representing all three stages of V's sexuality and gender identity development throughout the show's duration to date, we examine potential shifts in the discourse surrounding their coming-out process.

To do this, we focused on a Reddit discussion forum dedicated to *The Umbrella Academy*, r/UmbrellaAcademy. We chose Reddit for a number of reasons. First, Reddit.com is an important site for online fan discussion in general. In May of 2023, it was estimated that Reddit had 55.8 million daily users and well over a billion monthly users, making it one of the most popular websites on the world wide web[21]. The r/UmbrellaAcademy subreddit is a popular (172K members) online community hub for fans of *The Umbrella Academy*. In addition, its existence predates the advent of the television series by years, as it functioned (and continues to function) as a site for discussion about the broader *Umbrella Academy* fictional world, beginning with the comics and adding discussion of the television series when it became relevant. Our focus was on fan discourse around representations in the television series, so we used the dates of each season's release to guide which posts and conversations we looked at.

Using an interface built specifically for Reddit, submissions and comments dating back to the release date of the first season were collected from the r/UmbrellaAcademy subreddit. We analyzed how frequently new posts were made so that we could identify the times when fan discourse was at its peak. As expected, activity peaked in three-month periods around the release date of each new season of the television program. Using these isolated periods of activity, we created three separate blocks of fan discourse, each representing discourse that occurred within three months of the release of a season of episodes of the television program (2019, 2020, 2022). Overall, we ended up analyzing 98,670 comments from 6,622 Reddit submissions.

To ensure we had a dataset that spoke specifically to discussions of the character V, we filtered the data to only include submissions that included at least one of V's names (Vanya or Viktor) or one of many words, both positive and negative, that had to do with LGBTQ identities (such as transition, bisexual, queer, etc.). Submissions were included in this category if there was at least one occurrence of any of the words of interest. Additionally, we created a dataset that included submissions that did not reference V or LGBTQ identity. Doing so allowed us to analyze not only how discussions pertaining to V on the r/ UmbrellaAcademy subreddit changed over time, but also to compare those changes to changes in the rest of the subreddit. This approach, while not allowing us to capture nuances of rare or one-off comments, allows conclusions about persistent or frequent patterns of discussion in the subreddit as a whole.

ANALYSES OF *UMBRELLA ACADEMY* FAN DISCOURSE

We analyzed online fan discourse on r/UmbrellaAcademy using three computational tools to allow for a comprehensive exploration of changes in topic and tone throughout the three- season arc of Umbrella Academy. Each of the three tools we used is a version of natural language processing and allows for an in-depth exploration of the content and tone of large bodies of online discourse (for more details about the tools we used for this analysis, see https://osf.io/zh4bc/). Essentially, we used topic modeling to explore how often collections of similar words occur throughout and across bodies of text. These collections of words are used to infer "topics" or themes. Then, we conducted a analysis for these conversations that were happening for each season of the show. We looked at how closely connected individual words are to other individual words—how often they both appear in the same phrases or documents. This allows us to look at what other words frequently came up in discussion when fans talked about V. Lastly, we examined the sentiment (i.e., the positivity or negativity) of online discourse surrounding V's character and LGBTQ themes.

At this point, you are probably either dreading or really looking forward to a bunch of numbers and details of our analysis. Either way, you're in luck. We have left the nitty-gritty details out of this chapter, but we created an online database for those of you who are interested. The details are available here: here: https://osf.io/zh4bc/.

WHAT TOPICS WERE FANS TALKING ABOUT?

The results of the topic analysis showed four interpretable topics across the three seasons' worth of data we had collected: topics consistent with discussions of 1) relationships between/among characters 2) core plot points, such as the apocalypse; 3) Reddit utility, with words reflecting Reddit functionality such as upvoting; and 4) show-watching emerged across all seasons. There was apparent variation in topics across the three seasons. For season 1, prominent topics had to do with relationships among characters and major plot points. For season 2, these same two topics were central, but there was a noticeable discussion of Reddit functionality. Lastly, for season 3, prominent discourse topics included Reddit functionality, character relationships, and core plot points. These topics highlight the character and relationship-focused discussions that make up the bulk of the discourse present on the r/UmbrellaAcademy platform.

We also took a closer look at topics that pertained directly to V by examining the topics of all posts that made a specific reference to V or LGBTQ language. In season one, the most prominent topic of comments including V was V's familial relationships; this was apparently driven by discussions of V's relationships and interactions with specific siblings. In season two, topics of V- inclusive comments dealt with either familial relationships and contentions or V's relationship with Sissy and her family. Lastly, the prominent topics of comments that mentioned V in season 3 were rooted around the name Vanya, not Viktor. Here, the prominent topic had to do with words that seemed to allude to Page's gender transition in 2020.

WHAT WORDS WERE FANS USING?

Looking at the specific words used within discussions of V, we found that in season 1, V's name was most closely associated with words demonstrating their familial relationships, specific names of siblings (e.g., Luther, Allison, Klaus, etc.); mystical powers (e.g., power); and plot and show-related words (e.g., time, show, apocalypse). In season two, the single word most commonly associated with V's name was power. As with season 1, words discussing V's relationships with family (e.g., Klaus, Allison, Ben, etc.) were common. In addition, words reflecting V's romantic relationship in season 2 (e.g., Sissy and love) were among the most common connections. Words related to the show itself were also popular (e.g., make, season, character). In season three, the character V was once again most often associated with words alluding to familial relationships (e.g., Allison, Klaus, Luther, etc.). V was also linguistically connected to show-related words (season, show, make, etc.) and words about V's ability or the show's key plot points (e.g., power, kill, time). Finally, the link between the words "Viktor" and "Vanya," likely representing posts or comments that explicitly reference V's transition, were only the eighth most common link for either word in season 3.

HOW DID FANS FEEL?

By comparing means sourced from each activity period and their associated seasons (i.e., seasons 1, 2, and 3), we were able to examine the sentiment or tone of the comments that did and did not contain mention of V and compare them across time. First, we looked at the emotional tone of all comments from each season that did NOT mention V or LGBTQIA at all. For season 1, the average tone was relatively positive valenced. Seasons 2 and 3 had slightly lower tone scores (for more detail in how these scores were calculated, see https://osf.io/zh4bc/) indicating that discussions from this season were still positive, but less so than previous seasons. Across the three seasons analyzed, the tone of fan comments became more negative over time.

Next, for comparison, we analyzed the tone of just the comments that included mention of V or LGBTQIA words. Once again, there was a decline in the overall sentiment scores across time from Seasons 1 to 3. In season 1 and 3, the net tone was still positive, but in season 2 tone of discourse was more negative for V and LGBTQIA topic. Overall, the comments that included mention of V and LGBTQIA terms were more negative than comments that did not.

WHAT DOES IT ALL MEAN?

In light of past responses to canonical infidelity around identity in comic/cinematic universes and hyper-critical, negative fan- sparked phenomena like Gamergate, we set out to explore changes in fan discourse around the character of V from *The Umbrella Academy*. Our expectation was that we would observe some combination of both reactionary and progressive responses to V's identity development, especially in regard to the canonical infidelity of Viktor's transition in season three[22] [23]. However, our results did not indicate any substantial pattern of reactionary responses to the character's sexual and gender identity development across the show's three seasons. Instead, that development was acknowledged as just another element of a program that was focused mostly on the complexities of sibling relationships and world-ending superpowers.

Results from topic modeling indicated that prominent topics of fan conversations that included the character V were mostly related to relationships with other characters or Elliot Page's (not V's) transition in season three. Results from the semantic network analysis replicated and clarified the results from our topic model, indicating that V was discussed mostly in the context of character relationships and of their powers. Notably, these are central foci of the show; *The Umbrella Academy* is at least as much a familial relationship drama as it is anything else, and the characters' powers tend to be used as devices to talk about character and relationship development. When fans talk about V online, they talk about what the show is about.

No fundamental differences were seen in the broad trends of discourse around V across the three seasons, suggesting that discourse surrounding the character V did not change in drastic ways even while V's sexual and gender identity developed over the course of the show. Differences that were observed reflected new plot elements, as when mentions of Sissy and her family, V's quasi-family for much of Season 2, take their place alongside the persistent mentions of V's original adoptive family in the persons of her siblings. V's transition was certainly not entirely absent; during Season 3, fans mentioned "Viktor" and "Vanya" in close proximity to each other with substantial, though far from overwhelming, frequency. But the absence of any meaningful co-occurrence of either name with slurs, insults, or denigrating language is noteworthy. Again, fans mentioned V's transition, but when they talk about V, even in Season 3, they seem to be talking principally about the substance of the show—his relationships, his abilities, and the things that happen to him.

There were differences in tone across discourse from all three seasons of the show. Discourse grew more negative as the show progressed. However, we can only speculate as to why. It may be that Season 1, hewing more closely to canonical material, engendered more positive evaluations from fans. Almost certainly, there were fewer fans engaged in the discourse during the first season. It is also the opinion of one author that the show has grown progressively more grim across the three seasons. After all, Season 1 may conclude with the end of the world, but substantial parts of Seasons 2 and 3 deal with what happens *after*; much of Season 1 can be viewed through a hopeful lens that is largely snatched away for Seasons 2 and 3. If this is a widely- shared perception, then discourse around each season, even were it strictly descriptive, would be expected to be progressively more negative in tone as well. It is plainly not the case that the increasingly negative tone is attributable to changes V undergoes, because the tone becomes more negative even in comments that make no mention of V whatsoever.

We did find that comments that included mention of V or LGBTQ words were more negative (or less positive) in tone than other comments. We found little evidence to suggest that this was driven by fan negativity about LGBTQ issues, however. Instead, there is ample reason to believe that the difference is attributable simply to more negativity about the character V and their plotlines. First, in season 1, when V presents as a heterosexual cis-gendered woman, comments about V were still more negative than comments in general. Second, our topic modeling and semantic network results did not indicate that words reflecting bigotry, discrimination, or, meaningfully, identity were discussed frequently in direct relation to the character V. Finally, across all three seasons of the show, V is associated with a lot of the darkest, most negative plot points. In season 1, V attempts to kill her family, slits her sister's throat, murders the family's sentient, avuncular, chimpanzee butler, and brings about the end of the world twice. Twice! V is also the object of systematic child abuse in season 1 and government torture in season 2. In fan discourse during season 2, we do see that discussions of V and LGBTQ topics were significantly more negative than discussions of just V. Given our previous findings, it is likely that this is driven by the negative plotlines associated with V's relationship with Sissy (cheating, secrecy, Sissy's abusive husband, etc.) and not anti-LGBTQ hate from fans. Instead, it is clear that conversations about V are going to have a negative tone because the character's storyline has a negative tone.

Ultimately, then, the best way to characterize overall fan discourse around V's sexuality and gender identity development in *The Umbrella Academy* is as acknowledgment without notable judgment. When V engaged in a lesbian relationship during Season 2, that relationship was talked about, but with no particular rancor or stigmatization. When V came out as male in Season 3, the change was acknowledged by fans, but with no consistent negative association. In fan discourse around *The Umbrella Academy* on Reddit, discussions about V are about their relationships, their powers, and their role in the story.

While V's sexual and gender identity development were present topics in online fan discussions, these discussions were not notably homophobic or negative. In many ways, fans reacted to V's identity development in similar ways to V's own family in the show: acknowledgment and acceptance. In essence, our analysis illuminates contemporary fan culture's capacity for nuanced engagement with complex explorations of character identity within popular media, even when this identity development is not present in the original source material. This speaks to a growing trend of acceptance and inclusivity within fan communities (or at least *this* fan community), in which characters like V are embraced for their complexity as a character and role in a given narrative rather than judged for individual characteristics such as gender and sexuality.

ADDITIONAL INFORMATION

Graphs and visualizations from our topic models and network visualizations are stored in an OSF repository and can be accessed via this link: https://osf.io/zh4bc/

NOTES

1. Netflix. (2022). *Global top 10*. Netflix Top 10 - Global. Retrieved December 12, 2022, from https://top10. netflix.com/ tv?week=2022-06-26
2. Clark, T. (2019, April 16). *Netflix says 'The Umbrella Academy' was watched by 45 million households in the first month, and it's been renewed for season 2*. Business Insider. Retrieved December 12, 2022, from https://www. businessinsider.com/netflix-renews-the-umbrella-academy-for-season-2-details-2019-4
3. Netflix. (2022). *Global top 10*. Netflix Top 10 - Global. Retrieved December 12, 2022, from https://top10. netflix.com/ tv?week=2022-06-26
4. Wibrinda, P. M. (2021). Rethinking the 'truth of identity: dissecting queerness and emo subculture in Netflix's *The Umbrella Academy*. *Rubikon: Journal of Transnational American Studies, 8*(2), 139-152.
5. Ibid

6. Sepinwall, A. (2022, June 23). *Here's how "The Umbrella Academy" handled Elliot Page's transition -- and why it was the right call.* Rolling Stone. https://www.rollingstone. com/tv-movies/tv-movie-features/umbrella-academy-elliot-page-transition-season-3-1369326/

7. Meyers, S. (Host). (2021, May 13). Elliot Page opens up about his transition and incorporating it into The Umbrella Academy [Television broadcast]. Late Night with Seth Meyers. NBC. https://www.youtube.com/ watch?v=9yOYCzbxwGY

8. Taylor, L. D. (2015). Investigating fans of fictional texts: Fan identity salience, empathy, and transportation. *Psychology of Popular Media Culture, 4*(2), 172 - 187. https:// doi.org/10.1037/ppm0000028

9. Bentley, F. R. (2017, June). Understanding secondary content practices for television viewing. In *Proceedings of the 2017 ACM International Conference on Interactive Experiences for TV and Online Video* (pp. 123-128). https:// doi.org/10.1145/3077548.3077554

10. Semrush (2023). *Top 100: The most visited websites in the US.* www.semrush.com/blog/most-visited-websites

11. Lua, A. (2023, March 30). *21 top social media sites to consider for your brand -.* Buffer Library. https://buffer. com/library/social-media- sites/#15-reddit-430-million-maus

12. Chaney, K., & Liebler, R. (2007). Canon vs. fanon: Folksonomies of fan culture. *Media in Transition 5: Creativity, Ownership and Collaboration in the Digital Age.* http://works.bepress.com/ raizelliebler/10/.

13. Meyer, M. D. (2020). Black Panther, queer erasure, and intersectional representation in popular culture. *Review of Communication, 20*(3), 236-243. https://doi.org/10. 1080/15358593.2020.1778068

14. Ibid

15. Sackl, C. (2022). Screening Blackness: Controversial visibilities of race in Disney's fairy tale adaptations. In U. Dettmar & I. Tomkowiak (Eds.) *On Disney: Deconstructing images, tropes and narratives* (pp. 81-96). Springer Berlin Heidelberg.

16. Ibid

17. Schiappa, E., Gregg, P. B., & Hewes, D. E. (2006). Can one TV show make a difference? *Will & Grace* and the parasocial contact hypothesis. *Journal of Homosexuality, 51*(4), 15–37. https://doi.org/ 10.1300/J082v51n04_02

18. Bond, B. J. (2021). The development and influence of parasocial relationships with television characters: A longitudinal experimental test of prejudice reduction through parasocial contact. *Communication Research, 48*(4), 573–593. https://doi.org/10. 1177/0093650219900632

19. Cleland, J., Magrath, R., & Kian, E. (2018). The internet as a site of decreasing cultural homophobia in association football: An online response by fans to the coming out of Thomas Hitzlsperger. *Men and Masculinities, 21*(1), 91–111. https://doi.org/10.1177/ 1097184X16663261

20. Mortensen, T. E. (2018). Anger, fear, and games: The long event of #GamerGate. *Games and Culture, 13*(8), 787-806. Page 787. https://doi.org/10.1177/1555412016640408

21. Turner, A. (2023). Reddit user base & growth statistics: How many people use Reddit? (May 2023). www. bankmycell.com/blog/ number-of-reddit-users/

22. Proctor, W., & Kies, B. (2018). On toxic fan practices and the new culture wars. *Participations, 15*(1), 127-142.

23. Massanari, A. (2015). #Gamergate and The Fappening: How Reddit's algorithm, governance, and culture support toxic technocultures. *New Media & Society, 19*(3), 329-346. https://doi.org/10.1177/ 1461444815608807

PROTAGONISTS, VILLAIN PROTAGONISTS, AND MORALITY

ARIENNE FERCHAUD, PHD

L et's talk about morality. There is a theory in communication science referred to as the Affective Disposition Theory [1], which states that the impressions we form about a character's morality determines whether we will like or dislike that character. This theory explains why we all hate Joffrey in Game of Thrones (he seems to have no morality) but love Jon Snow (he seems to have high morality) despite the fact they both commit awful acts of violence. Alas, that is the wrong fandom and also is an example of how this idea – affective disposition theory – is often discussed out of context of the larger story in which these actions are taking place. A show like *The Umbrella Academy*, which features seven protagonist characters (i.e., the Hargreeves siblings), complicates these disposition formation models. Luther, Diego, Allison, Klaus, Five, Ben, and Viktor are all deeply flawed, yet usually sympathetic, characters. Their behaviors are sometimes difficult to parse, morally speaking, and often conflict with the actions and behaviors of their siblings.

How, then, can we explore their behaviors—and the connections that viewers build with them—in context of the larger narrative? The goal of this chapter is to explore existing models of affective disposition theory and its expansions in the context of the narrative of The Umbrella Academy to highlight the importance of context in understanding why we love (or love to hate) our favorite Hargreeves' children.

AFFECTIVE DISPOSITION THEORY: A THEORY OF MORALITY

Affective disposition theory (ADT) has been used by scholars to explain why viewers enjoy (or do not enjoy) stories of various types, including comedy, drama, and even sports spectatorship[2]. As we are talking about the Umbrella Academy, naturally our discussions will focus on the enjoyment of drama. Notably, drama here does not refer to content that is purely dramatic in nature, that is, content with dark, serious overtones, but content that falls broadly into the genre of drama. While I recognize that genres can overlap significantly— and *The Umbrella Academy* is certainly comedic at times—focusing on drama as a genre helps to simplify our understanding, given that humor introduces additional variables to the equation.

At its simplest, ADT argues that whether or not we enjoy the media we are consuming comes from the judgements we make about the righteousness of the story's outcomes[3]. When characters we like are rewarded, we enjoy the story. When characters do good, we like them. When characters act immorally, we begin to dislike them[4]. When characters we hate receive their comeuppance, we celebrate. Put another way, we as viewers carefully examine character actions and make our judgements accordingly. If their actions are moral, we form positive opinions about the character. If they are immoral, we form negative opinions about the character. The way the stories then proceed, or the narrative outcomes, then determine whether we like the story as a whole – good characters should be rewarded, while bad characters should be chastened.

The way we feel towards the different characters in our favorite stories is what drives the feeling of suspense. For characters that we like, we feel apprehensive when the story suggests they may fail, especially when that failure seems particularly likely. Likewise, when it seems that an antagonist may triumph over the heroes we've bonded over, suspense is heightened. If there is no suspense, well, then the story may be seen as boring or dull[5].

But what if a character acts morally at times, and immorally at others (i.e., Klaus)? What if a character acts immorally, but for a good reason (i.e., Vanya/Viktor)? Further, it is a rare narrative that involves only a singular character. What about a story that features seven, each with questionable morality?

THE MORALITY OF THE HARGREEVES SIBLINGS

There is no doubt that, by the time we meet the Hargreeves siblings in the present day of the Netflix original series, they are all troubled in different ways. Over the course of the first season, their various traumas run deep, leading them to act in ways that are not always moral.

LUTHER—"I NEVER WANTED TO BE THE BAD GUY."

At the beginning of season one, Luther arrives at Sir Reginald's funeral after a long stint on the moon, where he has been watching for threats to the planet. He is the one most attached to the idea of the Umbrella Academy; he is the one who most believes in his father's mission. Over the course of the first season, Luther is forced to confront the idea that his father, whom Luther has places on a pedestal, was a bad father. Luther's entire tenure on the moon was nothing more than a way for Reginald to keep Luther away. Once Luther learns this, he spirals, and in his attempts to hold on to his own feelings of righteousness, he ends up leading the charge in locking Viktor away, ultimately leading to the very apocalypse the siblings are trying to prevent.

Could Luther be seen as moral? Perhaps, at times. He does devote himself to trying to save the world, and is perhaps the closest to the "superhero archetype." Archetypical superheroes are said to be fundamentally moral with a selfless mission to protect others and fight evil[6] (Ke Jinde, 2022). Certainly, Luther sees himself that way. Though he does betray Viktor, locking him away as he tries to ask the siblings for help, Luther does so because Viktor had nearly killed Allison. In his mind, at least, locking Viktor away was the best way to prevent further harm.

Season two and three see a change in Luther. He pulls away from the superhero archetype. When the siblings are transported back in time to Dallas in the 1960s, his main concern is not to save the world, though Five certainly thinks it should be. Rather, he seems more interested in forming legitimate bonds with his siblings, apologizing to Viktor and casting aside the role of the superhero. In doing so, Luther pulls away from a hyper moral stance that simultaneously makes him more and less moral. While he becomes less concerned with the fate of the world throughout seasons 2 and 3 of the show, he also begins to treat his siblings and others better than he ever has. Rather than perpetuating the harmful number system that Reginald enforced on the children, he finally begins to understand how terrible Reginald was and begins to become a better sibling.

DIEGO—"I CAN'T BELIEVE I GOT SHANKED BY MY OWN FATHER."

Diego, though far more caustic in his general demeanor, also fulfills part of the superhero archetype. Throughout season 1, he acts as a Batman-like vigilante, acting alone to investigate Five's donut shop massacre and, later, the death of his former partner, Detective Patch. He does this at the expense of his own personal life. In season 2, this evolves as he tries to avert the assassination of John F. Kennedy, finding himself committed to an asylum as a result. Throughout Season 2 and 3, he softens, especially through his relationship with Lila. While Diego does strive to do good, he is, at times, unpleasant to be around due to his abrasive personality. He is violent, preferring to fight before trying to talk things out. At the same time, he is fiercely loyal to his siblings and Lila, and in season 3, when he believes that Stan is his son, he strives to be a good father—the kind of father that Reginald wasn't.

Diego's morality, like that of his siblings, is complicated. In his role as a vigilante, he aims to do good. Our first images of adult Diego in the Netflix original show him rescuing a family from a home invasion. In that sense, he is decidedly moral. In the second season, he is so committed to saving JFK from assassination that he winds up in an asylum. Yet he is also brash and, at times, deeply unlikeable. He is rude to his siblings and doesn't seem to have much care for them—at least on the surface. Throughout the series, he, like Luther, begins to let go of the hypercompetitive spirit that Reginald always enforced, allowing him to soften and show genuine care for his siblings.

ALLISON—"EVERY TIME I BUILD A NEW LIFE FOR MYSELF, YOU END THE WORLD AND TAKE IT FROM ME."

Allison is, perhaps, the sibling with the biggest swing in the morality of her behavior. At the beginning of the show, she is the sibling that others seem to get along with best. It is clear that she loves her siblings, and she is kind to Viktor when the others either ignore him or are actively hostile toward him. Throughout the first two seasons, she tries to avoid using her rumor powers, as she does not wish to manipulate others, even when it would help. However, Allison undergoes more trauma more than any of the other siblings. As a black woman, she suffers greatly when the siblings are transported back to 1960s Dallas. Further, at the end of season 2, she chooses to leave her husband Ray, in the past to return to her daughter in the present, only to realize in season 3 that her daughter has been erased from the timeline. As a result, Allison begins to act in increasingly immoral ways, rumoring Luther and then teaming with alternate timeline Reginald to betray her siblings. Although she ultimately realizes the error of her ways, she is ultimately rewarded for her immoral actions at the end of season 3, finding herself in a reality in which she is reunited with both Ray and her daughter. Her most morally reprehensible act is rewarded.

KLAUS—"I WANNA BE NUMB AGAIN."

Throughout the series, Klaus is a "comic relief" character. He is easy going and fun, but his abilities trouble him. He uses illicit substances to dampen his ability to see the dead, who constantly harass him. His addictions lead him to act in selfish ways. In fact, he inadvertently causes the events of the first season—and thereby the entire series—when he steals a valuable-looking box to sell, discarding the journal that leads Harold Jenkins down his corruption of Viktor.

Throughout season 2, Klaus is shown to be somewhat neglectful of his non-familial relationships. When he and Ben are transported back to the 1960s, he uses his powers in conjunction with Ben to convince a group of older women that he has mystical powers. Through manipulation and, at times, abuse of his relationship with Ben, he amasses enough followers to start a cult called Destiny's Children. While he is not necessarily malevolent in his cult leadership (for more on this, see Chapter 7), he does shape his followers' beliefs based on his own whims. When he tires of this new role, he abandons his followers.

Additionally, as he is the only one who can see and talk to the deceased Ben, he is Ben's only source of social support. At times, he is selfish in this relationship, which is by nature one-sided. He even tells the siblings in season 2 that ghosts can't time travel, further depriving Ben of a relationship with his living siblings. These actions are highly immoral in nature; his selfishness harms Ben, especially when the pair are living in 1960s Dallas. He begins to treat Ben as a means to an end—a way to perpetuate his cult, rather than a beloved sibling. Further, his desire to be loved by Reginald leads him to trust

Reginald in season 3, ultimately leading his siblings to trust a man who most certainly should not be trusted.

FIVE—"WONDER IF IT'S TOO LATE TO BE UN-ADOPTED"

Of all the siblings, Five is often the one most interested in the fate of the world. Season 1 reveals that Five, in a fit of overconfidence, accidentally trapped himself in the future, just after a world-wide apocalypse seems to have wiped out humanity. There, he lives with no one but a mannequin he names Dolores for company, until the Temps Commission finds and recruits him to become a time-traveling assassin.

As a member of the Commission, Five obediently kills the Commission's targets in order to maintain the timeline, a job which he does only until he is able to control his own time travel abilities enough to return to the present day to try and avert the apocalypse that initially left him alone for decades.

Five's goals are certainly noble and he almost certainly perceives his actions to be led by a strong moral compass. Throughout all three seasons of the show, he seeks to end various world- ending threats. However, he tries to accomplish his goals without involving his siblings, which often has disastrous effects. Further, of all the Hargreeves siblings, Five is the most bloodthirsty. He is shown killing people in incredibly violent ways. In a season 2 sequence, he murders several high-ranking members of the Temps Commission in a deal with the Handler, even though these individuals do not appear to be opposing him directly. He does this to try and return his siblings back to the present day, but these actions allow the Handler —someone who has shown to be antagonistic to the siblings and their goals—to take control of the Commission.

While Five acts to protect both his family and the world, his methods are violent. He possesses a fair amount of arrogance when talking to his siblings, dismissing them and their traumas, as he feels he, as the oldest (given his years of life after the apocalypse), has more experience. Thus, it is difficult to call him a truly moral character.

BEN—"ALL THE REST OF THIS, THESE YEARS WITH KLAUS. IT'S ALL BEEN GRAVY."

The Ben of the first two seasons is by far the sibling with the strongest morals. In fact, it is implied that his death is what causes the siblings to split in the first place; without his kind, calming influence, the others fall to their own vices. He is even shown to be reluctant to use his powers to kill, even when the situation calls for it. Though he is dead through the first two seasons, he strives to help Klaus—the only sibling who can interact with him—become a better person. At the end of season 2, it is he who averts the 1960s apocalypse, which he does by empathizing with Viktor, calming him down enough to avert tragedy.

The Ben of season 3 is an entirely different character. He exists only in the present caused by the Umbrella Academy Hargreeves siblings' meddling in the 1960s. This version of Ben, having grown up in an entirely different family, with different siblings, is highly competitive, striving always to be "Number One." He is, at times, vicious to his siblings in the Sparrow Academy, going overboard in a sparring match against Jayme seemingly only to flex his superior fighting skills.

This version of Ben lacks the deceased Ben's kindness and familial love. He is also incredibly jealous, first of the fact that he is considered Number Two, not Number One, of the Sparrow Academy, and later of the bond that the Umbrella Academy siblings seem to have. Even when he does come together with the Umbrella Academy to stop Sir Reginald's plans, his demeanor grates on the others, and he is not well liked by his siblings, either in the Sparrow Academy *or* in the Umbrella Academy.

VIKTOR—"I ENDED THE WORLD TWICE, AND YOU...YOU'RE JUST MEAT IN SPANDEX."

Viktor begins the Netflix series believing that he, unlike his siblings, has no powers. He was constantly neglected by Sir Reginald, and told that he was not special. Over the course of the first season, his isolation from his siblings leads him to connect with Harold Jenkins, who manipulates Viktor into realizing that he *does* have powers. In fact, of all the siblings, Viktor's powers are perhaps the most potent. After being manipulated for the entire season, he lashes out at Allison—nearly killing her. He destroys the Umbrella Academy home and kills Pogo, one of the siblings' caretaker and one of the few characters who always treated Viktor kindly. Ultimately, Viktor's powers cause the apocalypse. Though he doesn't destroy the world on purpose, he does destroy the world, forcing the siblings to jump back in time.

Throughout season two, Viktor goes on a quest of self discovery, learning to love himself in a way that wasn't possible before. In doing so, he forms a connection with Sissy and her son, Harlan, and ultimately saves Harlan's life when he nearly drowns. In doing so, Viktor accidentally imparts some of his own powers into Harlan, which leads to disaster in season 3.

Further, Viktor very nearly causes another apocalypse in the 1960s when he is captured and tortured by the government. Additionally, his saving of Harlan results in the deaths of all the Umbrella Academy's mothers before they can be born, resulting in a paradox that destroys the world and plays into Sir Reginald's rather dubious plans. Yet, for all the destruction that Viktor causes, he doesn't *intend* to harm others. The question therefore arises of whether the morality of his actions is determined by his intentions, or by the outcome.

WHY DO WE LIKE THE HARGREEVES DESPITE THEIR SHIFTING MORALITY?

While Affective Disposition Theory (ADT) states we love or hate a character based on their morals alone, this is insufficient to explain why viewers find the exploits of the Hargreeves siblings so compelling. If, as ADT suggests, viewers constantly monitor character behavior to determine liking of said characters, then the most liked characters should be the most moral. However, this is not necessarily the case. While the ghostly version of Ben from Seasons 1 and 2 is clearly the most moral of the family, it is Klaus and Five that are generally the most well-liked (for more on this, see Chapter 5).

Part of the problem lies in the fact that, despite occasional adherence to the superhero archetype, the Hargreeves siblings may be more accurately described as anti-heroes, or characters who display both heroic and villainous traits[7]. Thus, morality is *not* the only determining factor for the formation of affective dispositions, but that identification with characters may be important[8].

In this context, identification refers to the viewer's ability to internalize the thoughts, feelings, and behaviors of a given character[9]. In other words, identification measures the degree to which a viewer can "walk in the character's shoes." If we think of characters like Klaus and Five, perhaps there are aspects of their character background and motivations that viewers can identify with. Klaus, for instance, is easy-going, always wanting the best for his siblings despite occasionally feeling that they don't care about him as much as he does. These traits may make him relatable, despite the fact that viewers lack his ability to communicate with ghosts. And, while Five may be a murderous, and at times, cold, assassin, he also displays a great deal of loyalty and annoyance that many experience with their siblings. Thus, it is possible that we are able to look past their immoral actions because we're able to identify with them.

But why do we switch from appraising characters based on their morals, to potentially judging how well we identify with them when the characters are antiheroes? One argument is that viewers have seen stories before, hundreds of thousands of them, in fact. As a result, we build up an array of so-called story schemas – or frameworks – to help us understand the stories we consume. These schemas may include things like genre conventions or literary tropes, and they prevent the viewers from coming into any story with a completely blank slate[10].

When a viewer first encounters *The Umbrella Academy*, it is abundantly clear from the first few minutes of the first episode that it is a fantastical, somewhat surreal show featuring a group of superpowered siblings. Thus, when they are introduced to the characters that serve as the protagonists, viewers already have expectations about those characters. Because the Hargreeves siblings are set up as the heroes of the story, the audience treats them as such. Thus, when they behave in immoral ways, we don't necessarily immediately discount the characters; we look for ways to excuse their behavior (this process of excusing immoral behavior is known as moral disengagement[11]).

Even though the Hargreeves siblings are, at times, immoral, they are the heroes of the story. As such, we hold pre-conceived ideas (or schemas) about how we expect them to behave. When they act counter these expectations by doing bad things, we look for reasons to explain this behavior away. When Five slaughters the Commission members in season 2, we may excuse him by suggesting that his actions were necessary to help his siblings (though this massacre proves to make things worse in the end). Alternatively, we may argue that the Commission agents, who regularly send time-traveling assassins to murder sometimes innocent people, are worse than Five, who merely carried out orders. And When Kalus starts a cult we say, "Oh, well that's just Klaus."

Research has even shown that no matter the justification for the immoral actions, this kind of moral disengagement leads to more positive impressions of these characters and greater enjoyment[12]. Notably, identification is a key factor here; characters that we strongly identify are the characters whose actions we are likely to excuse.

It is also important to note that much of the discourse about impression formation with characters assumes specific character roles within the context of their stories. The *protagonists* of the story are assumed to be good, based on pre-existing genre schemas, while the *antagonists* are presumed to be bad[13] . While there are often subversions of these expectations, such as the hero antagonist[14] and the villain protagonist[15], even these tropes suppose that the roles of the characters within the story are fixed. The protagonist is the protagonist, and the antagonist is the antagonist. What is fascinating about *The Umbrella Academy* is that, among the Hargreeves siblings, the roles of protagonist and antagonist constantly shift.

Certainly, some of the siblings are always positioned as protagonists. It would be very difficult, for instance, to characterize the ghost of Ben to as an antagonist in any sense. However, some of the siblings *do* act against the interests of the others. In season 1, the siblings discover that Viktor is the one to cause the apocalypse. Viktor kills Pogo and destroys their home, pushed to extremes by the manipulations of Harold Jenkins and perceived betrayals by his siblings, especially Luther. At this stage, Viktor becomes an antagonist, though his thoughts, feelings, and behaviors may be understandable.

Additionally, Viktor's turn to darkness seems very much understandable, or even justified. For his entire life, he is told by Sir Reginald that he is not special—a lie perpetrated in part by a young Allison using her powers to make Viktor forget his powers. Viktor's siblings also constantly discount him, shutting him out of conversations and excluding him from decision- making because of his apparent lack of powers. When he does finally go to them for help, they lock him away. As such, though he does act as an antagonist for the last few episodes of the first season, it's not done maliciously.

CONCLUSION

Another example of this switch in character role is Allison in season 3. Throughout the series, Allision is portrayed as one of the more stable of the Hargreeves siblings, though she does have her manipulative moments. This changes rapidly in season 3, when Allison's traumas build her to the point where she is hostile toward her siblings at the best of times and actively opposes them at the worst. She helps Sir Reginald, a decision which nearly kills the Hargreeves siblings, but ultimately gets her what she wants; a life with both Ray and her daughter.

While thinking about the morality of a character is a useful way to think about why we like certain characters, hate others, and love to hate others still, it does not account for the full complexity of story structure or—perhaps more importantly—character relationships. Characters do not exist in a vacuum, free of context. They live within the confines of a narrative. They act not only for themselves, but for others. For the Hargreeves siblings, much of *The Umbrella Academy* revolves around not only the fantastical, world-ending events they find themselves trying to oppose, but also the way they bond with their dysfunctional family.

And dysfunctional they certainly are, each suffering greatly from the traumatic upbringing they all endured together. Their trauma, at times, leads them to act in ways that are antithetical to the archetypical superhero. They're not necessarily hyper moral characters who put the needs of others above themselves. They are frequently selfish, caustic, and unpleasant. Though they ultimately do strive to do good, they often do so by committing highly immoral actions.

Our traditional understandings of narrative enjoyment often rely on characters behaving in accordance with prescribed character roles; the protagonist is good (or at least justified) and the antagonist is bad. The Hargreeves siblings subvert this understanding.

In exploring the morality of these characters, we can see that study into entertainment media must take into account context. It's important to understand how characters relate, not only to the story, but to each other. Only then can we have a full understanding of characters as unique as the Hargreeves siblings and the stories they inhabit.

NOTES

1. Raney, A.A. (2017). Affective Disposition Theory. In P. Rössler, C.A. Hoffner and L. Zoonen (Eds.), *The International Encyclopedia of Media Effects*. Wiley.
2. Raney, A. A. (2006). The psychology of disposition-based theories of media enjoyment. In J. Bryant & P. Vorderer (Eds.), *Psychology of Entertainment*. Routledge.
3. Raney, A. A. (2004). Expanding disposition theory: reconsidering character liking, moral evaluations, and enjoyment. *Communication Theory, 14*(4), 348–369. https://doi.org/10.1111/j.1468-2885.2004.tb00319.x
4. Zillmann, D. (2000). Basal morality in drama appreciation. *Moving Images, Culture, and the Mind*, 53–63.
5. Raney, A. A. (2011). Media enjoyment as a function of affective dispositions toward and moral judgment of characters. In K. Döveling, C. von Scheve, & E. Konijn (Eds.), *The Routledge Handbook of Emotions and Mass Media* (pp. 166–178). Routledge.
6. Ke Jinde, K. (2022). The superhero archetype as an auxiliary class in Marvel's Avengers Movies. *Essence & Critique: Journal of Literature and Drama Studies, II*(II), 54–69.
7. Jonason, P. K., Webster, G. D., Schmitt, D. P., Li, N. P., & Crysel, L. (2012). The antihero in popular culture: life history theory and the dark triad personality traits.

Review of General Psychology, 16(2), 192–199. https://doi. org/10.1037/a0027914

8. Janicke, S. H., & Raney, A. A. (2018). Modeling the antihero narrative enjoyment process. *Psychology of Popular Media Culture*, 7(4), 533–546. https://doi.org/10. 1037/ppm0000152

9. Cohen, J. (2001). Defining identification: A theoretical look at the identification of audiences with media characters. *Mass Communication & Society, 4*(3), 245–264.

10. Raney, A. A. (2004). Expanding disposition theory: reconsidering character liking, moral evaluations, and enjoyment. *Communication Theory, 14*(4), 348–369. https://doi.org/10.1111/j.1468-2885.2004.tb00319.x

11. Sanders, M. S., & Tsay-Vogel, M. (2016). Beyond heroes and villains: Examining explanatory mechanisms underlying moral disengagement. *Mass Communication and Society, 19*(3), 230–252. https://doi.org/10.1080/ 15205436.2015.1096944

12. Krakowiak, K. M., & Tsay-Vogel, M. (2011). The role of moral disengagement in the enjoyment of real and fictional characters. *Int. J. of Arts and Technology, 4*, 90– 101. https://doi.org/10.1504/ IJART.2011.037772

13. Raney, A. A. (2004). Expanding disposition theory: Reconsidering character liking, moral evaluations, and enjoyment. *Communication Theory*, 14(4), 348–369. https://doi.org/10.1111/j.1468-2885.2004.tb00319.x

14. Hero Antagonist. (n.d.). TV Tropes. Retrieved January 23, 2024, from https://tvtropes.org/pmwiki/pmwiki.php/ Main/ HeroAntagonist

15. Villain Protagonist. (n.d.). TV Tropes. Retrieved January 23, 2024, from https://tvtropes.org/pmwiki/pmwiki.php/ Main/ VillainProtagonist

SYSTEMS, ROLES, AND COPING: A CASE STUDY OF THE HARGREEVES' FAMILY

SHANE TILTON, PHD

One of the main draws of the mind-bending world of *The Umbrella Academy,* beyond showing the downsides of being a superhero, is how Gerard Way and Gabriel Bá peeled back the glossy exterior to reveal a troubled family system simmering just beneath the surface. The closed doors of Sir Reginald Hargreeves' mansion hide the emotional baggage and traumas that come with their extraordinary lives. When Reginald plucked the seven children from different walks of life at birth to fulfill his vision of the perfect masked protectors, he never considered how to provide the emotional support needed for children to grow with some measure of normality in society. Rather than making his house a home, Sir Reginald Hargreevs created a pressure cooker of unaddressed emotions and shattered relationships

The Umbrella Academy provides a compelling case study for family trauma as it vividly portrays a troubled family system's intricate dynamics and lasting effects. As a viewer, we must witness the consequences of Sir Reginald's emotional neglect and the family's lack of healthy communication on top of the extraordinary pressure placed on the Hargreeves' children to fulfill their father's (and, by extension, the rest of society's) expectations. The audience witnesses the creation of deep-seated wounds that result in strained relationships, unresolved conflicts, and various psychological struggles. In the end, the Hargreeves children are left with an unresolved yearning for love and connection, as they grow up bearing the scars of feeling unseen and unimportant[1].

In this chapter, we use a family systems approach[2] to explore the relationships between the Hargreeves' children, Luther, Diego, Allison, Klaus, Five, Ben, Vanya/Viktor, and their father Sir Reginald (please note that Viktor will be referenced as Vanya/ Viktor throughout this chapter to denote the Dark Horse comic version of the character (Vanya) and who the character becomes in the later seasons of the Netflix television series (Viktor).) As a classic "troubled family system," we will explore the realities of how the Hargreeves' came to be a family of superheroes tasked with saving the world, but ultimately, while seeking the love and validation of their father.

FAMILY SYSTEMS THEORY

Family systems theory is rooted in the idea that the family unit is a complex social system where family members use whatever skills, interactions, and resources they have at their disposal in order to influence each other's behaviors as a collective whole, as opposed to individual members[3]. That is, the whole is greater than the sum of its parts. This approach is clear in the behavior of Sir Reginald who consistently acted in ways that suggested his children had less value as individuals than they did as a collective whole (e.g., locking Klaus in a tomb to deal with ghosts, Luther being injected with gorilla serum/having his body surgically replaced with that of a Martian gorilla, and Allison losing her hand to save her voice).

There are five key components of family systems theory: communication patterns, family life cycle, differentiation, triangulation, and family roles. Each of these components provide insight into understanding the family dysfunction of the Hargreeves' family as both individuals and a family and help us as the viewer better understand why the Hargreeves exhibit the previously mentioned struggle to express their emotions openly and honestly, leading to a buildup of tension, misunderstandings, and unspoken pain.

COMMUNICATION PATTERNS

Family systems theory places significant emphasis on communication patterns and how they shape relationships within the family. Patterns can be functional or dysfunctional. Functional communication is when family members communicate their thoughts and feelings freely with one another. Families who can do this, who have what is called a "high conversation orientation", are more likely to interact more, have more rewarding relationships with their family members, and make collective decisions. Not only that, but families with greater communication are also better equipped to handle family stress, have a closer touchpoint on the day-to-day lives of their family members, remember important family events (from the past and the future), display better collective problem solving, and have a shared language[4].

Anyone who has seen the Netflix adaptation of *The Umbrella Academy* knows that a lack of communication is perhaps the most defining trait of the Hargreeves family. Not only are many of the siblings physically isolated, by being unreachable throughout the course of the series (though, time travel will do that), they are also emotionally isolated. When the siblings return for Sir Reginald's funeral in the opening episode of the Netflix Series (S1, E1) we are met with a collection of individuals who seemingly have no emotional or social connection at all. They are seemingly disjoined, disconnected, and together, show little collective grief for the loss of their patriarch. This is not the kind of communication – social or emotional support – one would expect to see upon reuniting at a parent's funeral. This is the first insight we get into the dysfunctional history of communication and connection among the Hargreeves family. We see this when Diego resents Vanya from showing up back to the Sir Reginald mansion after his death after the release of Vanya/Viktor's "tell- all" autobiography, Luther's suspicion of the rest of family being the cause of Sir Reginald's death, and Klaus' mocking celebration of the death in Sir Reginald's office.

While a lack of communication is a common trope used in popular culture (for example, other television shows, movies, video games, graphic novels, etc. the Hargreeves tend to frame a few cases that highlight their low conversation orientation. The strongest of these cases is how it seems that in the Netflix series that the various Hargreeves are unreachable and isolated throughout the course of the series. The lack of cell phones within the series represents a technological isolation among the Hargreeves with the additional effect of rare displays of pathos within their interactions promotes the concept of emotional isolation (e.g. the fighting after Sir Reginald's funeral in the first episode of the Netflix series and the the second issue of the *Apocalypse Suite* graphic novel series). Once again from a narrative perspective, the focus on action in an action comic series is logical. The family system theory would point to these actions as a representation of the low conversation orientation of the Hargreeves with a focus on the physical to resolve issues (as opposed to other forms of engagement).

Healthy communication patterns are not just about communicating freely but also exhibiting what is referred to as communication conformity, which is the "homogeneity of attitudes, values, and beliefs"[5] with family communication practices. Essentially, it is the shared values across family members and the extent to which those values are *valued* across members of the family unit. One of these shared values could be listening and being polite. Communication conformity in this example would be that everyone waits their turn to speak and uses kind words to address one another. If one family member is telling a story, everybody waits until the right times to respond. Families with high conformity orientation tend to prioritize conflict avoidance among family members, focusing on being obedient to parents and other adult authority figures.

While it can be argued that the mental manipulation powers that Allison has can force the rest of the Hargreeves siblings to conform to Allison's wishes and that Sir Reginald's genius could outsmart his adopted children into conformity, it is hard to find examples of times that the siblings actually conformed to their other family members. The only clear example is when they were fighting crime and were organized tactically in their battles with the bank robbers, The Commission, the zombie-robot Gustave Eiffel, and various other villains that they faced as a collective. Because they have low conformity and low conversation, the Hargreaves fall into what is called "laissez-faire" communication style. Koerner & Fitzpatrick (the developers of family systems theory) explain this communication style based on:

> Their communication is characterized by few and usually uninvolving interactions among family members that usually concern only a limited number of topics. Parents in laissez-faire families do believe that all family members should be able to make their own decisions, but, unlike parents in pluralistic families, they have little interest in their children's decisions, nor do they value communicating with them[6].

That "little interest in their children's decisions" marks the relationship between Sir Reginald and his adopted children. In every measured way, Sir Reginald only seems to care that his children can shape the world in his specific and controlling vision of how it should be and run. Referencing the children as mere numbers and superhero monikers instead of giving them normal children's names is the simplest example of expressing little interest in them. Most of the siblings claiming those "normal" children names when they became adults reveals the last of the five significant concepts.

FAMILY LIFE CYCLE

The family life cycle points to how family members transition into various roles as they age, and the family structure evolves due to these changes. Understanding where individual family members exist within the family life cycle presents unique challenges and tasks that ordinary families must navigate. The negotiation of the family life cycle is often grounded in the various developmental tasks that are required (e.g., emotional support, caretaking, and direct engagement) for the family to maintain cohesiveness among its members[7]. In contrast, it is hard to argue that the Hargreeves were a conformist group; their role as children was in line with being Sir Reginald's foot soldiers. Their collective trauma due to Sir Reginald's psychologically destructive training and the death of Ben broke the siblings from this role. They morph into the previously listed family roles due to breaking away from the rest of the family.

DIFFERENTIATION

Differentiation refers to the ability of individual family members to maintain their sense of self while remaining emotionally connected to the family as a cohesive unit. This particular aspect of the family unit relates to the boundaries the family sets among themselves and a barrier they create between themselves and the rest of the outside world[8].

A great example of the rigid boundaries within the Hargreeves' world can be seen in the relationship between Allison and Luther. Allison could have found happiness with Patrick or Raymond. However, Allison seemed to not have the willpower needed to maintain any meaningful relationships away from the Hargreeves. She created rifts in her marriage to Patrick by using her powers on her daughter to ease her to sleep after a long day (S1, E8) and also made the decision to join her family instead of staying in the same timeline as her second husband Raymond (S2, E10). Her need to maintain her bonds with the Umbrella Academy seemingly keeps Allison from finding happiness apart from her adoptive family.

Throughout the stories of *The Umbrella Academy*, we see Allison struggle to create a separate sense of self (or differentiate) from her family. However, there is one exception during her time in the 1950s timeline. Allison thrived during this time, she marries Raymond, opens a hair salon, and is an active participant in the Civil Rights Movement. This is a clear example of successful differentiation – Allison has created and maintained a sense of self outside of her family unit.

TRIANGULATION

Triangulation, like when two friends arguing and asking another friend to pick a side, happens when conflicts between two people involve a third person or issue. Families sometimes use triangulation to deal with stress, like when Mom asks Dad to talk to their child about homework because she's worried about their grades. In larger families, like the Hargreeves siblings in *The Umbrella Academy*, it's common for one sibling to involve another in their disagreement to help ease tension or avoid confronting the issue directly[9].

An example of triangulation can be seen in S1 E8 when Luther intervenes between Allison and Vanya/Viktor and chooses to lock Vanya/Viktor in a soundproof room after they hurt Allison with their powers. Luther made this decision in haste in an effort to reduce the anxiety of the family as a group (with the exception of Vanya/Viktor) in dealing with the ramifications of Vanya/ Viktor's newly developed powers.

Another example can be found in the pilot when Allison supports Vanya/Viktor's homecoming back to the mansion over Diego's objections. Allison had to put aside her shock of her sibling's revelations and family secrets being shared to the public in Vanya/Viktor's autobiography. Allison "taking" Vanya/Viktor's side by allowing them to stay was in service of keeping the family together during a period when most families would grieve collectively the loss of another family member.

FAMILY ROLES

Family roles are exactly what it sounds like. It refers to the specific part each family member plays within the family system[10]. These roles are typically defined by basic demographic factors, such as gender, age, and birth order. The roles in the Hargreeves' family are, of course, not so straightforward. For example, Sir Reginald seems to have numbered the children based on the overall usefulness of the children to completing his mission of changing the world in his image or, perhaps, his ability to influence and control them[11]. The family roles in the Umbrella Academy can also be framed by the superhero names the children were originally assigned by their creators, Gerard Way and Gabrielle Bá:

- Luther aka "Spaceboy" points to both being the youngest person to ever become an astronaut and his role of that being isolated on the moon for years
- Diego aka "The Kraken" points to him also isolate himself (in this case underwater for hours on end), and his ability to be a terror (with his control of knives [from the Netflix series and the first issue of the *Apocalypse Suite* graphic novel series])
- Allison aka "The Rumor" points to her ability to control reality by speaking it into existence and acting as a voice for those that did not have one during her time in the 1960s
- Klaus aka "The Seance" points to his emphatic nature as the one that both can connect with the dead and broadcasting his thoughts to others via the airwaves
- Five aka "The Boy that Disappeared"/"The Boy" points to both being a wunderkind prophet that can travel through

time (i.e., a boy genius) and his genetic modification to never age

- Ben aka "The Horror" points to his ability to possess other worldly monsters under his skin and the collective trauma that the family experiences when he his killed
- Vanya/Viktor aka "The White Violin" points to their musical talent and them being an instrument of the apocalypse during the first season finale

While these names may have been part of their public personas, they also provide insight into the roles they play within their family. Specifically, the living Hargreeves siblings point to traditional family roles as defined within the family systems literature12, 13, (Ben is not included in this grouping, as his return was with the Sparrow Academy).

- Luther playing the classic "hero" role as he is a high achiever to please his adopted father,
- Diego playing the classic "scapegoat" role as he is the one that challenges Luther's role of leader most often and tends to act out the most,
- Allison playing the classic "caretaker" role as she will bend reality to protect her family,
- Klaus playing the classic "mascot" role as he often inject himself with a flare for entertaining the family,
- Five playing the classic "mastermind" role as the person most likely to get what they want (i.e., using the ability to travel through time to escape his problems), and
- Vanya/Viktor playing the classic "lost child" role as they were excluded from most of the siblings' conversations due to the belief that they lacked any superpowers.

COPING AND ADAPTING IN A FAMILY SYSTEM

A tangential aspect of the family system theory is how the various listed concepts associated with the theory help scholars better understand the role that coping and adapting play in the family setting. Coping and adapting tend to take two different forms as it relates to dealing with stress. Coping deals with thoughts and behaviors that are used to manage and minimize the impact that stressful situations and stimuli can have on a person's daily lives[14]. An example of a coping mechanism in the family setting can be when a family member is stressed out about an upcoming test in school that they discuss that stress with a parent, who can talk the family member through the aspects that are causing the stress[15].

Adapting falls in line with making fundamental changes to one's daily actions in order to minimize the triggers associated with stress. One example of an adaptive strategy is going on more walks as a both a change in lifestyle and developing routines that build resilience to stress over a period of time[16].

Understanding the importance of coping and adjusting within the family system requires a keen acknowledgement of those five aspects of the family system model and their impact on the development of individual family members. Those communication patterns taught at the family level gives each family member a template for how communication can be used to either alleviate (in the form of addressing the point of stress with other family members) or aggravate (in the form of lashing out at other family members when dealing with stress) the stressful condition. Recognizing where one is within the family life cycle means that family members adjust how they approach stressful situations based on their maturity to the situation.

Having a good sense of differentiation allows family members to avoid codependency as a coping mechanism (in the form of always deferring to the family and not being able to individual deal with stress)[17]. Knowing effective triangulation skills prevents one of the family members being "the correct one" when conflicts arise. Finally, knowing the family role that one plays in the family system allows one to find comfort in the "conformity of expectations" (in the form of knowing one's place in the family).

Both coping and adapting are grounded in the idea that they are attempting to adjust one's focus, energy, and attention away from stressors by focusing on good social psychological practices in the form of coping mechanisms or effective actions to move around the feeling of being stress in the form of adaptive strategies[18, 19]. The Hargreeves siblings have found some measure of comfort in applying those coping mechanisms and adaptive strategies that work best for them.

COPING AND ADAPTING THE HARGREEVES' WAY

The Hargreeves siblings have proven throughout the course of this chapter, their Dark Horse graphic novels, and Netflix series that their focus, energy, and attention are often dealing with tensions and stress that the average family system would not experience. The dramatic parts of the Hargreeves' life makes for an outstanding work of fiction, but would absolutely physically and psychologically damage those families without superpowers (a.k.a. everybody reading this chapter most likely came from a family that did not have superpowers). Even without the shared social experiences of a superhuman family, there are lessons that the Hargreeves siblings can share with the rest of the population to understand how to cope and adapt to stressful situations in a family system..

Luther can teach us that we can accept failure as part of the normal process of life. He was so focused on never being wrong and disappointing his father in the earlier season that he forced himself to be a hyper-masculine leader that literally aped his father's wishes. Luther lets go of that need toward the third season and finds himself in a better place with the rest of his family.

Diego can teach us that there must be some level of balance

between rebelling against all of the social institutions that exist in society and conforming to the authorities that one would find in the community. He would often find the straightforward approach to problems but would be impulsive in his attempts to solve those problems (e.g., saving Vanya/Viktor at the expense of saving JFK from assassination). This inability to maintain control and restraint harms his ability to communicate emotionally with the rest of his family effectively.

Allison can teach us that manipulating family members will always have some cost. Her powers cost her a marriage and her child. Her manipulations later in life were often in service of continuing her caretaker role. Unlike the traditional techniques one would use in this role (e.g., using verbal engagements to emulate typical parent-child interactions, hovering over other siblings to pay attention to others' experiences and problems, & catering to others' whim at the expense of personal happiness and self-care), Allison used her superpower to shortcut this process[20].

Klaus can address how getting sober means confronting the aspects of trauma, especially as his trauma is grounded in his superpower. His drug use was an ineffective coping mechanism, as it led to a self-numbing state as opposed to actively addressing other means of controlling his power and the ramifications of the death of Ben (as he can still see and talk to Ben throughout the series). The series gets to a central societal truth via the correlation between childhood trauma, substance addiction, and other mental health issues. Beyond Klaus' action being described as hedonistic and attention-seeking, it becomes a way for Klaus to avoid (ever so temporarily) the painful aspects of his reality and childhood experiences.

Five highlights how merely choosing escapism presents more issues in the future. His ability to escape any situation to a time and place outside his control means that he is trapped in a narrative outside his control (i.e., where he ends up) and ultimately manages to avoid the traumatic experience. At the same time, he maintains emotional distance from the rest of the family. This emotional distance prevents Five from making deeper connections with his family.

Vanya/Viktor finally points to the need to be authentic to oneself in the face of dealing with trauma. For all of the criticism of how the Netflix show treats non-white characters' storylines in the earlier episodes and marginal improvement in the later episodes21,22, it seems to have incorporated a LGBT narrative in the form of Viktor's story in a meaningful way within the family dynamic. The second episode of the third season (i.e., "World's Biggest Ball of Twine") allows the family to be "introduced" to Viktor as a whole person for the first time and the family accepting him for who he is in a manner described in Out Magazine[23]:

> The Umbrella Academy is showing that accepting someone's transition, especially if that someone is in your family, doesn't have to be the end of the world. In fact, the Umbrellas have dealt with the end of the world, and their reaction to Viktor's transition is the opposite.

The lessons from the "living" Hargreeves can give viewers of the show some guidance of how to cope with trauma and stress in the modern world.

CONCLUSION

Way and Bá's depiction of the imperfect superhero group is not a new construction. Elements of *The Watchmen*, *The Boys*, and *Doom Patrol* can be found in *The Umbrella Academy*. Even the exploration of trauma from the superhero vantage point is a common narrative technique among these four series[24]. What makes *The Umbrella Academy* unique among the four series is the development of the adopted family structure being the primary mode of socialization that the main characters have throughout the series. Sir Reginald plays the role of the Monocle and unwillingly plays the role of father to the Hargreeves. This lack of a traditional family structure (among other social institutions that the Hargreeves have no connection with in their society) forces the siblings to redefine the family system in a non- traditional way, thus becoming one of the foundations of the various storylines for both the Netflix television series and the Dark Horse comic series. The children must cope and adapt to their adopted family without the benefit of the typical social support that most families would have.

NOTES

1. Shaughnessy, K. (2021). Gothic Academy: Horror and crookedness in a haunted household. In L. Anders (Ed.), *The Force of The Umbrella Academy: Essays on Voices and Violence in the Comics and Netflix Series* (pp. 10-31). McFarland, Incorporated.
2. Bowen, M., & Kerr, M. E. (1988). *Family Evaluation*. W. W. Norton.
3. Ibid.
4. Koerner, F. A., & Fitzpatrick, M. A. (2002a). Understanding family communication patterns and family functioning: The roles of conversation orientation and conformity orientation. *Communication Yearbook, 26*(1), 36-65. 10.1080/23808985.2002.11679010
5. Koerner, A. F., & Fitzpatrick, M. A. (2002b). Toward a theory of family communication. *Communication Theory, 12*(1), p. 85
6. Ibid., p. 87
7. Gilligan, M., Stocker, C. M., & Conger, K. J. (2020). Sibling relationships in adulthood: Research findings and new frontiers. *Journal of Family Theory & Review, 12*(3), 305-320. 10.1111/jftr.12385

8. Manzi, C. (2014). Family Differentiation. In A. C. Michalos (Ed.), *Encyclopedia of Quality of Life and Well-Being Research* (pp. 2169-2170). Springer Netherlands.

9. Ross, A. S., Hinshaw, A. B., & Murdock, N. L. (2016, September 06). Integrating the relational matrix: attachment style, differentiation of self, triangulation, and experiential avoidance. Contemporary Family Therapy, 38, 400-411. 10.1007/s10591-016-9395-5

10. Zagefka, H., Jones, J., Caglar, A., Girish, R., & Matos, C. (2021). Family roles, family dysfunction, and depressive symptoms. *The Family Journal: Counseling and Therapy for Couples and Families, 29*(3), 346-353. 10.1177/1066480720973418

11. Tyler, A. (2022, June 22). Umbrella Academy: What the order of the team's numbers actually means. Screen Rant. Retrieved June 16, 2023, from https://web.archive.org/web/20230328171541/ https://screenrant.com/umbrella-academy-team-numbers-mean- actually-order/

12. Verdiano, D. L., Peterson, G. W., & Hicks, M. W. (1990). Toward an empirical confirmation of the Wegscheider role theory. *Psychological Reports, 66*, 723-730.

13. Zagefka, H., Jones, J., Caglar, A., Girish, R., & Matos, C. (2021). Family roles, family dysfunction, and depressive symptoms. *The Family Journal: Counseling and Therapy for Couples and Families, 29*(3), 346-353. 10.1177/1066480720973418

14. Algorani, E. B., & Gupta, V. (2023, April 24). *Coping Mechanisms.* StatPearls [Internet]. https://www.ncbi.nlm.nih.gov/books/ NBK559031/

15. Lazarus, R. S., & Folkman, S. (1984). *Stress, Appraisal, and Coping.* Springer Publishing Company.

16. Fteiha, M., & Awwad, N. (2020). Emotional intelligence and its relationship with stress coping style. *Health Psychology Open, 7*(2), 2055102920970416.

17. Lampis, J., Cataudella, S., Busonera, A., & Skowron, E. A. (2017). The role of differentiation of self and dyadic adjustment in predicting codependency. *Contemporary Family Therapy, 39*, 62-72.

18. Schwarzer, R., & Schwarzer, C. (1996). A critical survey of coping instruments. In M. Zeidner & N. S. Endler (Eds.*), Handbook of Coping: Theory, Research, Applications* (pp. 107-132). Wiley.

19. Tilton, S. (2012). First year students in a foreign fabric: A triangulation study on Facebook as a method of coping. ProQuest LLC.

20. Zagefka, H., Jones, J., Caglar, A., Girish, R., & Matos, C. (2021). Family roles, family dysfunction, and depressive symptoms. *The Family Journal: Counseling and Therapy for Couples and Families, 29*(3), 346-353. 10.1177/1066480720973418

21. Ahmad, M. (2022, June 28). The Umbrella Academy and Its Treatment of Marginalized Characters. Nerdist. Retrieved June 18, 2023, from https://web.archive.org/web/20230323085221/ https://nerdist.com/article/the-umbrella-academy-approach-race- issues-sparrow-academy-allison-ben-diego-lila-netflix/

22. Truffaut-Wong, O. (2022, June 28). The Boys and Umbrella Academy are Finally Doing More with Their Marginalized Characters. Polygon. Retrieved June 18, 2023, from https://web.archive.org/web/20230324185712/ https://www.polygon.com/23185393/the-boys-umbrella-academy- characters-season-3

23. Rude, M. (2022, June 22). Viktor's Storyline in 'Umbrella Academy' Is a Trans TV Game Changer. Out Magazine. Retrieved June 18, 2023, from https://web.archive.org/web/20220831075504/ https://www.out.com/television/2022/6/22/viktors-storyline- umbrella-academy-trans-tv-game-changer

24. Cedro, C., & Speakman, B. (2021). An "Extra-ordinary" Adaption: exploring time and trauma in *The Umbrella Academy*. In L. Piatti- Farnell (Ed.), *The Superhero Multiverse: Readapting Comic Book Icons in Twenty-First-Century Film and Popular Media* (pp. 181-198). Lexington Books.

ABOUT THE EDITOR

I heard a rumor that Arienne Ferchaud is an assistant professor in the School of Communication at Florida State University. Her research revolves around new and emerging media technologies and entertainment, especially with regards to video games, social media, and television streaming.

Her work has been presented at numerous national and international conferences and has been published in journals such as *Psychology of Popular Media, Computers in Human Behavior, and Journal of Gaming and Virtual Worlds*. She has also appeared on livestreams, podcasts, and non-academic panels to discuss all things entertainment. Her favorite Umbrella Academy characters are Five and Klaus, but she concedes that Allison has the best powers.

ABOUT THE AUTHORS

Kelly Chernin, PhD is an assistant professor in the Department of Communication at Appalachian State University. Her research explores the implementation of strategic communication strategies to promote sustainable social change. She has researched pro-democracy movements in Hong Kong and China, better approaches to disseminating refugee narratives, and how local governments can facilitate more efficient phosphorus management. She is currently the editor of the *Journal of Public Interest Communications*. She is also interested in starting her own benevolent cult in the future to have followers pay off her college loans. Her favorite Umbrella Academy characters are Klaus and Ben.

Emory S. Daniel Jr., PhD is an associate professor in the Department of Communication at Appalachian State University. His research specializes in parasocial relationships/interactions, gaming, interactive media, strategic communication, and advertising pedagogy. His research has been published in outlets such as *Journal of Interactive Advertising, Communication Research Reports, Game Studies, Psychology of Popular Media, and Computers in Human Behavior*. His favorite Umbrella Academy Character is Five.

In the shadowy corridors of academia, **Andreas Fahr** emerges not as your typical professor but as a mysterious figure shrouded in enigma. Known to many as "The Handler," he navigates the murky waters of media studies at the University of Fribourg in Switzerland with an air of intrigue. Behind the guise of a scholarly facade lies a mind deeply entrenched in the secrets of media manipulation and its effects on the human psyche. With a focus as sharp as a precision-engineered umbrella, The Handler delves into the intricate motivations and habits that drive media consumption, unraveling the tangled web of parasocial contact and dissecting the very fabric of cognitive and emotional responses to media content. His journey through the labyrinth of academia led him to the halls of the University of Munich in Germany, where he obtained both his habilitation and his doctorate degree, honing his skills and sharpening his intellect to become the master manipulator of media mysteries that he is today. In the world of media studies, The Handler reigns supreme, his expertise casting a shadow over all who dare to tread in his footsteps. His favorite Umbrella Academy character is The Handler.

Jennifer Fuller, PhD is a Communications and Training Lead at Sierra 7 where she works to provide high-quality training and communications support for business and technology professionals at Veterans Affairs (VA). She also provides Shakespeare quotes at key moments in work events. Previously, she was a college professor serving at Jackson State University, Idaho State University, and Warner University. Her previous book, *Dark Paradise*, was a work of literary criticism that explored the Pacific islands through the lens of nineteenth- century literature. Her love of islands (and science fiction) is a theme that carries through much of her work, including her latest co-authored book *Beyond Atlantis: Islands of Imagination*. She is currently working on a project about the first missionaries to the Pacific islands. . .and also one about a Victorian detective and her wolf partner. When not writing, she likes to binge *The Witcher* and *Sweet Tooth* between marathon sessions of Stardew Valley. Her favorite Umbrella Academy character is Pogo.

Jasmine Heyward is a researcher, writer, and multimedia storyteller at New America's Better Life Lab. With previous experience as a reporter, K-12 educator, researcher, and lab coordinator, they bring a diverse perspective to their work exploring how stress, systemic oppression, and mental illness intersect with family dynamics. Heyward works across media disciplines, producing policy-focused research, opinion pieces, and essays for the Better Life Lab's flagship projects and contributing to guides, toolkits, and presentations for Hollywood executives and creators through the Lab's Entertainment-Focused Narrative and Culture Change Practice. Heyward's contributions to this initiative are the latest products of a decade of research on depictions of trauma, mental illness, and marginalized community experiences across fictional media. They hold an MA in digital and interactive storytelling for which they studied the utility of forced blind choices in video games to help players better understand experiences of repeat victimization and complex trauma. Their favorite Umbrella Academy character is Klaus.

Michelle Möri orchestrates her academic symphony as a research assistant at the University of Fribourg in Switzerland. Her journey toward a Ph.D. in media psychology is a harmonious exploration of the audience members' interactions and relationships with fictional media characters such as the Hargreeves siblings from The Umbrella Academy, Emily from Emily in Paris, or Thomas Shelby from Peaky Blinders. Thereby, she is armed with a BA and MA in media and communication research, coupled with expertise in German language and literature. Within the academic tapestry of the University of Fribourg, she navigates the motivations driving media consumption and explores the effects it exerts on individuals. In her quest for knowledge and pursuit of understanding people's media use, she embodies a symphony of relentless pursuit, weaving together the threads of fiction and reality. Her favorite Umbrella Academy Character is The White Violin.

Petrana Radulovic is an entertainment reporter at Polygon, where she covers movies, TV, and everything in-between. With a particular focus on animation and fandom culture, she's appeared on a few podcasts including Buzzfeed Daily, CBC, and Business Wars.Petrana graduated from the University of Florida with degrees in English and Computer Science (and is shocked by which one she ends up using the most these days). When she's not writing for work, you can usually find her ... well, still writing in some way, shape, or form. In her free time, she also admins an online collaborative creative writing group. Her favorite Umbrella Academy characters are Lila and Diego.

Sofia V. Rhea is currently a PhD candidate in the Department of Communication at UC Davis. Her research focuses on how patterns and modes of media use can shape audience well-being, particularly among adolescents and vulnerable users. Rhea's current research focus is centered on fan community participation and well-being outcomes. She is particularly interested in how the communal aspects of fanship, such as online fan community interaction, may influence well-being outcomes in a variety of populations. In all, Rhea is a fan of all things fan related. Her favorite Umbrella Academy Character is Séance.

Laramie Taylor, PhD is a professor of Communication at the University of California, Davis, where he studies mediated communication, especially narratives. His research tends to emphasize how people use (and are influenced by) media in ways that relate to social identity, perception, and interaction. As part of this overall project, he is endlessly interested in fans, especially fans of fictional narratives, studying the personality traits and motives that make people more or less likely to identify as a fan. His favorite Umbrella Academy character is Spaceboy.

Shane Tilton. PhD is the Irene Casteel Endowed Chair for Education, Professional, and Social Sciences and an Associate Professor of Multimedia Journalism at the Ohio Northern University.

Tilton is also a Fellow for the Ohio Northern University Institute for Civic and Public Policy. He was named the 2018 Young Stationers' Prize for his work advancing journalism and communication scholarship and education in United States higher education for nearly two decades. He was the first American in the more than six century history of the Worshipful Company of Stationers and Newspaper Makers to earn such an honor. Tilton's research normally falls in the realms of collegiate game-based pedagogy, the psychological issues surrounding ludology, multimedia journalism's influence on society, social media engagement, and memetic communication practices. His work on social media and its connection to university life earned him the 2013 Harwood Dissertation award from the Broadcast Education Association. His last book "Meme Life" was awarded the 2023 Top Book Award from the National Communication Association's Human Communication and Technology interest division. His favorite Umbrella Academy character is The Boy.

ABOUT PLAY STORY PRESS

https://playstorypress.org/about/

Play Story Press™ is an open community publishing consortium of/by/for the field and our community. It is a diamond open-access academic publishing initiative in which contributors retain all their intellectual property. We work with our contributors in as timely a manner as possible so that we can share ideas that have impact and significance in our society.

Play Story Press is a culmination of 20 years of open-access publishing and collaborating with the community. Our founders started ETC Press in 2005 as an experimental open-access academic publishing imprint, and our success was a direct result of all the quality work written by our community. Inspired by this, Play Story Press is evolving to focus more on the community and field. The consortium comprises an exceptional group of partner organizations that will work together, shaping and supporting Play Story Press for the field and community.

Publishing with Play Story Press is a friendly, supportive and constructive process focused on encouraging the growth of quality scholarship in this field. Play Story Press is committed to publishing three types of work: peer-reviewed work (research-based books, textbooks, academic journals, conference proceedings), general audience work (trade nonfiction, singles, Well Played singles), and research and white papers. The common thread among these is a focus on issues related to stories and play as they are applied across various fields.

The concepts of story and play are broad and diverse—from entertainment and narrative to media studies and social studies, games and technology to health and enjoyment, education and learning to design and development, and more. Our authors come from a range of backgrounds. Some are traditional academics. Some are practitioners. And some work in between. Their ability to write about the impact of play and story and their significance in society ties them all together.

In keeping with our mission, Play Story Press uses emerging technologies to design all our books and on-demand publishers to distribute our e-books and print books through all the major retail chains, such as Amazon, Barnes & Noble, Kobo, and Apple. We also work with The Game Crafter to produce tabletop games.

We publish books but are also interested in the participatory future of content creation across multiple media. We are exploring what it means to publish across multiple media and versions. We believe this is the future of publishing, bridging virtual and physical media with fluid versions of publications and enabling the creative blurring of what constitutes reading and writing.

We don't carry an inventory ourselves. Instead, each print book is created when somebody buys a copy. Since the Play Story Press is an open-access publisher, every book, journal, and proceeding is available as a free download, we're partnering with open-access supporters to host our online repository, and we price our titles as inexpensively as possible because we want people to have access to them. We're most interested in the sharing and spreading of ideas. Authors retain ownership of their intellectual property. We release our books, journals, and proceedings under a Creative Commons license.

Play Story Press™ is an independent non-profit organization powered by input and involvement from the consortium, our contributors, and the community at large. This continues our innovations in publishing, and we invite people to participate. Together, we can explore and create the future of open academic publishing, sharing and spreading ideas and knowledge that can help change the world for the better.

www.ingramcontent.com/pod-product-compliance
Lightning Source LLC
Chambersburg PA
CBHW060508290526
45791CB00001B/317